The Greatest Possible Being

# The Greatest Possible Being

Jeff Speaks

OXFORD
UNIVERSITY PRESS

# OXFORD
UNIVERSITY PRESS

Great Clarendon Street, Oxford, OX2 6DP,
United Kingdom

Oxford University Press is a department of the University of Oxford.
It furthers the University's objective of excellence in research, scholarship,
and education by publishing worldwide. Oxford is a registered trade mark of
Oxford University Press in the UK and in certain other countries

First Edition published in 2018
Impression: 1

Published in the United States of America by Oxford University Press
198 Madison Avenue, New York, NY 10016, United States of America

British Library Cataloguing in Publication Data
Data available

Library of Congress Control Number: 2018939064

ISBN 978-0-19-882681-1

Printed and bound by
CPI Group (UK) Ltd, Croydon, CR0 4YY

*This book is dedicated to Elyse, Amelia, and Violet, who make every day wonderful.*

# Contents

# Introduction

In the spring of 2013, I taught a large lecture class at Notre Dame on the topic of 'Philosophical Theology.' The organizing idea for the class was to work through the Nicene Creed, considering as we went the best arguments for the incoherence of the central doctrines of Christianity laid out in that document.

Many of the toughest questions that quickly arise—about evil, about the doctrine of original sin, about judgement and the afterlife— are best pressed against the background assumptions that God is omnipotent, omniscient, and perfectly morally good. So I wanted some way to get the students to see why claims of this sort about God were plausible (whether or not the students themselves believed in God).

My idea was to follow what I thought of as a traditional line of thought: I would begin by introducing them to the idea of a greatest possible being, and then explain why, if God exists, it is plausible that God is the greatest possible being. I would then explain why, if there were a greatest possible being, it would be omnipotent, omniscient, and perfectly morally good.

But that lecture turned out to be harder to write than I thought. Despite what I thought was a consensus that there was a simple argument from the claim that God is the greatest possible being to the traditional attributes, I could not figure out how the derivation was supposed to work.

Four years later, I still can't. The first five chapters of this book explain why. Once one tries to make the argument suitably precise,

I argue, there is just no way to derive interesting claims about God from the principle that God is the greatest possible being.

This (still) seems to me to be very surprising. The form of argument one finds in Anselm and in much recent work in the philosophy of religion—that the greatest possible being must have every property which it is better to have than lack, and knowledge, power, and goodness are all better to have than lack, and so must all be attributes of God—is intuitively extremely compelling. I still have the uneasy feeling that I must be missing some way to make this intuitive argument work. But I've now been trying long enough to make it work that it seems worthwhile to publish the case against it.

Even if the principle that God is the greatest possible being cannot be used to derive the divine attributes, it might still have important theoretical roles to play. Recent work in the philosophy of religion has suggested two. The first is the role of setting the boundaries of the core of our concept of God—as telling us what properties of God are, so to speak, non-negotiable when theorizing about the divine attributes. The second, related role is the role of giving the meaning, and fixing the reference, of the name 'God.' In Chapters 6 and 7, I argue that the claim that God is the greatest possible being is similarly unsuited to play these theoretical roles.

After seven chapters of negativity, in Chapter 8 I make some positive suggestions about how to answer the questions which the claim that God is the greatest possible being has been used, unsuccessfully, to answer.

\* \* \*

Thanks to the John Templeton Foundation, which funded the year of leave from teaching during which most of this book was written. Thanks also to groups at the Center for the Philosophy of Religion at Notre Dame and the Center for the Philosophy of Religion at Rutgers, where I presented earlier versions of this material. The group at Notre Dame even had to suffer through it two times. This book has benefited from questions and comments from many people, but among those who deserve special mention are Brian Cutter, Cameron Domenico Kirk-Giannini, Sam Newlands, Mike Rea, Blake Roeber, and Meghan Sullivan.

# 1

# The Idea of a Greatest Possible Being

Other than the question of whether God exists, no question in the philosophy of religion and philosophical theology is more fundamental than the question of the divine attributes: the question, to put it in ordinary language, of what God is like.

How should we go about answering this question? One traditional view, which has received a significant revival over the last half-century, begins with the claim that God is the greatest possible being. This claim is most often associated with the name of St. Anselm, who in the second chapter of the *Proslogion* describes God as 'a being than which nothing greater can be conceived.' But this was, as others have noted, not an entirely novel claim.

In the Christian tradition, Anselm was notably preceded by Boethius, who asked

For since nothing can be imagined better than God, how can we doubt Him to be good than whom there is nothing better?[1]

which apparently presupposes that God is something than which no greater can be imagined. And Augustine wrote the following about our concept of God:

For when the one supreme God of gods is thought of, even by those who believe that there are other gods, and who call them by that name, and worship them as gods, their thought takes the form of an endeavor to reach

---

[1] Boethius, *Consolation of Philosophy*, X.

the conception of a nature, than which nothing more excellent or more exalted exists.[2]

Augustine's claim here is not quite as strong as the claim we find, implicitly in Boethius and explicitly in Anselm. Whereas Anselm claims

God is the greatest conceivable being.

Augustine claims only that[3]

God is the greatest being.

There is logical space to believe the second of these but not the first—though this space of course vanishes if one believes, as Anselm did, that the greatest conceivable being actually exists.

Both of these claims can be distinguished from a claim which one principally finds later in the tradition than Anselm, namely

God is the greatest possible being.

While from our vantage point it is natural to sharply distinguish this modal claim from the corresponding claim about conceivability, it would at least arguably be a mistake to read this distinction into the work of earlier thinkers. To my knowledge, no one until the modern period explicitly distinguishes between the claim that God is the greatest conceivable and the greatest possible being; the claim is invariably stated in broadly psychological terms, as the claim that God is the greatest thinkable, or imaginable, or conceivable being. But that hardly implies a preference for the psychological formulation over the modal one, given that it is also quite rare to find any explicit distinction between the conceivable and the possible before Descartes.[4]

---

[2] *On Christian Doctrine*, I.7.

[3] Though other passages in Augustine suggest the stronger claim, e.g. 'For no soul ever has been, or ever will be, able to conceive of anything better than you . . .' (*Confessions* VII.4).

[4] The earliest such discussion I know of relates to Descartes' claim in *Meditation* VI that 'if I have a vivid and clear thought of something, God could have created it in a way that exactly corresponds to my thought.' Criticism of this claim, especially

Even if we should not read a preference for psychological over modal formulations into past thinkers, we now clearly do have the resources to distinguish the claims that God is the greatest possible and the greatest conceivable being, and in what follows it will be important to keep them separate. If possibility implies conceivability but not the reverse, and the actuality implies possibility but not the reverse, these three theses can be ordered from logically strongest to weakest as follows: God is the greatest conceivable being, God is the greatest possible being, and God is the greatest being.[5]

## 1.1 From greatness to the divine attributes

Almost as old as our trio of claims is the attempt to derive from these claims more specific claims about the attributes of God. Anselm, as is well known, used the claim that God is the greatest conceivable being to, via the ontological argument, derive the conclusion that God has the property of existence. But he also used it to show, among other things, that God is 'just, truthful, blessed, and whatever it is better to be than not to be.'[6]

Just as the idea of God as the greatest conceivable (or possible or actual) being pre-dates Anselm, so does the idea of using this conception of God to derive more specific claims about God.[7] Plato has

from Arnauld, can at least be read as centering on the link between conceivability—the vivid and clear thought—and possibility. See his 'Fourth Objections,' in Cottingham et al. (1988), vol II, 140. By the time we get to Hume, the distinction is quite explicit— even if Hume thinks that 'whatever the mind clearly conceives, includes the idea of possible existence, or in other words, that nothing we imagine is absolutely impossible' (*Treatise*, I.II.ii), and hence that the conceivable and the possible are coextensive. See, for interesting discussion, Yablo (1993).

[5] Of course, there are, notoriously, many different senses of 'conceivable,' and for many of these it would be incorrect to say that possibility entails conceivability. There are, for example, presumably many possible scenarios which limited creatures like us cannot imagine. For other senses of 'conceivable,' the entailment will plausibly hold. The key point for now is simply that there are good senses of 'conceivable' on which some claims are conceivable but not possible, and this fact is one which the proponent of the thesis that God is the greatest conceivable being might exploit.

[6] *Proslogion* §V.    [7] For useful discussion, see Leftow (2011).

Socrates reason from the claim that the gods are the greatest possible beings to the claim that they are immutable:

Then it is impossible that God should ever be willing to change; being, as is supposed, the fairest and best that is conceivable, every god remains absolutely and for ever in his own form.[8]

And Cicero, following Zeno, reasons from the claim that the universe is the greatest actual being to the claim that the universe possesses every property which it is better to have than lack:

These arguments, for instance, which are expanded by modern Stoics, used to be compressed by Zeno as follows: 'That which exercises reason is more excellent than that which does not exercise reason; there is nothing more excellent than the universe, therefore the universe exercises reason.' In the same way it may be proved that the universe is wise, blessed, and eternal, for all objects that possess these qualities are more excellent than those which do not possess them, and there is nothing of greater excellence than the universe. By this means it will be proved that the universe is divine.[9]

The form of argument is a simple but powerful one: God is the greatest being; it is better to be $F$ than not-$F$; so, God must be $F$.

The mainstream of contemporary philosophy of religion is squarely within this venerable tradition. Philosophy journals for the last half century have seen many attempts to settle upon a list of the divine attributes, and to give more specific accounts of the traditional candidates: omnipotence, omniscience, goodness, eternity, and so on. It is unsurprising, given the nature of philosophy, that this discussion has not yielded much consensus. It is, however, quite surprising that such a general consensus has emerged that the way of answering questions about the attributes exemplified by the passages just listed is basically correct.

Here, to pick just one among many possible examples from this literature, is Thomas Morris:

---

[8] Plato, *Republic* II.  [9] Cicero, *On the Nature of the Gods*, II.7–8.

[W]e can represent schematically the development of a conception of a perfect being . . . In ascending order of greatness in metaphysical stature, God is conceived of as:

(1) conscious (a minded being capable of thought and awareness)
(2) a conscious agent (capable of free action)
(3) a thoroughly benevolent conscious agent
(4) a thoroughly benevolent conscious agent with significant knowledge
(5) a thoroughly benevolent conscious agent with significant knowledge and power
(6) a thoroughly benevolent conscious agent with unlimited knowledge and power who is the creative source of all else
(7) a thoroughly benevolent, necessarily existent conscious agent with unlimited knowledge and power who is the ontologically independent creative source of all else.

And here we have arrived at what, with its entailments, is the highest conception of all, the conception of a greatest possible or maximally perfect being.[10]

The method on display here—of deriving claims about God from the claim that God is the greatest, or greatest possible, or greatest conceivable, being—is often called 'perfect being theology.' The idea is nicely summed up by Murray and Rea, who say that the principle that God is the greatest possible being 'provide[s] us with a rule or recipe for developing a more specific conception of God.'[11]

To me, derivations of the attributes like the one just quoted have always seemed to have a slightly magical feel—as though a theological rabbit is being pulled out of a modal hat. If perfect being theology is a recipe, and perfect being theologians the chefs, then, like many great chefs, it seems to me that perfect being theologians have occasionally been less forthcoming about the ingredients, and exactly how they are supposed to go together, than they could have been. One of the main

[10] Morris (1987), 26.
[11] Murray and Rea (2008), 8. Morris (1991) uses the same culinary metaphor, saying that [GPB] is 'like the main element in a recipe for cooking up our idea of God in detail' (35).

things that I want to do in the chapters that follow is to try to lay out the method of perfect being theology—or, rather, a range of choices for how to think about that method—in more detail than has been done thus far.

## 1.2 The modal conception of God

Even if there are some unanswered questions about how exactly to understand the method of perfect being theology, there is no mystery about why that method has seemed to be so attractive to so many philosophers and theologians. One crucial question is—taking for granted that God exists—how much we can know about God by the use of reason alone, without reliance on revelation or the assumptions of individual religious traditions. And it might well seem that the method of perfect being theology promises an optimistic response to this question.

In order to get started on the project of deriving by reason alone the attributes of God, we need a starting point—some assumption about God which, independently of revelation and tradition, we can see to be true. And the claims that God is the greatest actual, or greatest possible, or greatest conceivable, being might seem to provide just the wanted starting point. Let's call this the *modal* conception of God—the conception of God as the best thing in some space of worlds (which might include just the actual world, just the possible worlds, or also conceivable but perhaps impossible worlds).

The modal conception of God is an attractive one for rational theology because it combines two features which are both difficult to combine and essential to the project of rational theology. The first feature is a kind of *neutrality*. The claim that God is the greatest possible being does not in itself say anything very specific about God—and this fact is part of what makes it an attractive starting point. It does not in itself say that God is powerful, or loving, or immutable—and hence is a claim which might, in principle, be endorsed by someone whether or not they find those claims about God initially plausible.

It is not hard to imagine people with radically different views of God finding common ground in the claim that God is the greatest possible being.

Indeed, on many views something stronger can be said. This is because many take 'God' to be a kind of descriptive name: a name which is either synonymous with a definite description, or incorporates significant descriptive elements. And a number of theorists have thought that the relevant description is something like 'the greatest possible being.'[12] If a view like this were correct, then the modal conception of God simply gives the content of 'God.' This would make the claim that God is the greatest possible being not just plausible, but literally analytic, since then it would be possible to transform it into a logical truth just by substituting synonyms for synonyms.[13]

The second feature is a kind of *productivity*. Despite its neutrality, perfect being theologians, following Anselm and others, think that the formula that God is the greatest possible being can be shown to entail various more specific claims about God. And this is, as we have seen, a quite plausible claim. It certainly seems as though we can see that some properties are better to have than lack, and it certainly seems as though these would have to be properties of the greatest possible being. And it is difficult, I think, to come up with another starting point for theological speculation which would better combine neutrality and productivity.

It is, however, important, to distinguish from the outset the modal conception of God from more substantive conceptions of God with which it can be conflated. Consider, for example, Leibniz's conception of God as the *ens perfectissimum*, where a perfection is 'every simple quality that is positive and absolute, or that expresses without any

---

[12] I discuss this sort of view of 'God' at length in Chapter 7.
[13] Here I ignore for simplicity the fact that sentences rather than propositions are the primary bearer of analyticity, and that the best candidate for an analytic truth in the vicinity would really be the conditional 'If God exists, then God is the greatest possible being.' I'll return to these issues when we turn to the semantics of 'God,' in Chapter 7.

limits whatever it expresses.'[14] The view of God as having all perfections, in this sense, is not the modal conception of God. If one starts with the view that God has all perfections, then, to figure out which are the divine attributes, one has to figure out which are the positive simple qualities. The principle that God is the greatest possible (or conceivable) being has no obvious role to play in this inquiry.

Of course, one might try to derive the claim that God has all perfections from the claim that God is the greatest possible being; one might try to derive, that is, Leibniz's view that God is the *ens perfectissimum* from the modal conception of God. That would be to go in for a kind of perfect being theology. But, while his name is often associated with the thesis that God is the greatest possible being, that strategy was clearly not Leibniz's. If it were, he would not have been so concerned to argue for the thesis that it is possible that the subject of all perfections exist. If we derived our list of perfections from the concept of a greatest possible being, then the compossibility of the perfections would be trivial.

This is not, of course, to deny that Leibniz endorsed the thesis that God is the greatest possible being. No doubt he did. But one can endorse this thesis without giving it the role in the determination of the divine attributes which it plays in perfect being theology.

## 1.3 Two steps to a perfect being theology

How do we move from the modal conception of God to a view of the divine attributes?

Perfect being theology is a procedure which aims to give us a principled way of making progress on the question of whether a given property $F$ is, or is not, among the divine attributes. Hence it must give us some way of completing the biconditional

$F$ is a divine attribute iff . . .

----

[14] Leibniz (1969), 167, cited in Adams (1994), 142.

in a way which is such that instances of the right-hand side of the biconditional are easier to evaluate than instances of the right-hand side of the uncontroversial but unhelpful

F is a divine attribute iff F is a property of God.

It is not hard to get some handle on how this should work. A first step is to pick as a starting point one of our three principles about God:

God is the greatest actual being.
God is the greatest possible being.
God is the greatest conceivable being.

Let's call this first choice point the choice of a *modal principle.*
These three modal principles will trivially entail, respectively,

F is a divine attribute iff F is a property of the greatest actual being.
F is a divine attribute iff F is a property of the greatest possible being.
F is a divine attribute iff F is a property of the greatest conceivable being.

Our question about the method of perfect being theology thus reduces to the question: how do we tell whether something is a property of the greatest actual, possible, or conceivable being?

The answer to this question is, I think, fairly straightforward. What the perfect being theologian needs is a condition on properties which is such that a property's satisfying that condition, together with the relevant modal principle, entails that God has that property. This condition will make precise the thought that the property is one which it is better to have than lack. Let's call a condition of this sort a *greatness condition.*

A pure version of perfect being theology will consist of one of the above modal principles, together with a greatness condition. Though the terminology is novel, the basic idea here seems to fit well with the way that the method of perfect being theology is often characterized by its proponents. The idea is that we begin with a claim about the greatness of God, point out that a certain property is (in a sense to be made precise) better to have than lack, and conclude that God has that property.

It should be uncontroversial, I think, that our greatness condition must satisfy the following two desiderata:

[Entailment]:   it should follow from the fact that a property $F$ satisfies the condition, plus the relevant modal principle, that $F$ is a property of God.

[Informativeness]:   it should be possible (without reliance on prior substantive claims about God) to see that some interesting candidates to be divine attributes satisfy the condition.

If a greatness condition did not satisfy [Entailment], it would not be doing the job for which it was introduced, since then the fact that a property satisfied the condition would not tell us anything about the divine attributes. If a greatness condition did not satisfy [Informativeness], it would never deliver an interesting result, and hence again would not tell us anything of interest about the divine attributes. (Obviously, satisfaction of this second desideratum will be a matter of degree.)

It is fairly obvious that one's choice of a greatness condition will depend on one's choice of a modal principle, since, for example, the fact that a property meets some condition might entail that it would be a property of the greatest actual being, but not that it would be a property of the greatest possible being.

If we think of a particular instance of perfect being theology as consisting of a modal principle and a greatness condition, then, two ways in which that instance can fail are by its greatness condition failing to meet [Entailment] or [Informativeness]. But there is of course another way in which it can fail: its modal principle can be false. One way to show that a modal principle is false is to provide a greatness condition which meets both [Entailment] and [Informativeness], but is also satisfied by properties which are not plausible candidates to be among the divine attributes. As we'll see below, our modal principles are not as beyond challenge as they are sometimes taken to be.

In setting things up in this way, it's important not to saddle the perfect being theologian with a commitment she need not take on.

Advocates of perfect being theology typically do not think that they have in hand, as Morris puts it, a 'fully mechanical procedure'[15] for deriving the divine attributes—a procedure which, without any further philosophical assumptions, will provide us the answer we want. This does not mean that there is something wrong with asking for a precise formulation of the method. But it does mean that we should not demand that our greatness condition be such that we should expect to be able to determine what falls under it without employing non-trivial philosophical assumptions about the relative greatness of various actual and possible beings, as well as assumptions about what is and is not possible. Of course, if those assumptions are trivially equivalent to the claims about God to be argued for—which, as we will see, is sometimes the case—this will be genuinely problematic.

## 1.4 Modal principles

In what follows it will be important to be clear about exactly when a property's satisfying a greatness condition, together with a modal principle, entails something about God. So it will be useful to introduce some notation so that the relevant claims can be stated as clearly as possible.

To give us a sense of how the relevant claims should look, there's no better place to start than §V of the *Proslogion*:

What are you, then, Lord God, than whom nothing greater can be conceived? But what are you, except that which, as the highest of all beings, alone exists through itself, and creates all other things from nothing? For, whatever is not this is less than a thing which can be conceived of. . . . What good, therefore, does the supreme Good lack, through which every good is? Therefore, you are just, truthful, blessed, and whatever it is better to be than not to be. For it is better to be just than not just; better to be blessed than not blessed.

Anselm's line of thought brings out two important points. The first is that when Anselm and others talk about properties which it is better

---

[15] Morris (1991), 41.

to have than to lack, what 'better than' expresses is in the first instance a relation between individuals rather than between properties. When we say that it is better to have than lack $F$, what we are saying is that the things which are $F$ are (in general, or all things being equal) better than the things that are not-$F$. It is not the abstract object, the property of justice, which is praiseworthy; it is the individuals which possess this property. (This is presumably why Anselm says 'it is better *to be* just than not just.') In what follows I will use '$>$' to express this relation of being greater than between individuals.

The second point is required by the fact that Anselm relies, not just on the claim that God is the greatest being, but also on the claim that God is the greatest conceivable being. And when we ask which individuals are greater than which other individuals, we will sometimes wish to compare the greatness of an actual individual with the greatness which some individual could have had, or can be imagined to have, but does not actually possess.

I will follow contemporary orthodoxy in using the apparatus of possible worlds to represent claims of this sort. So, for example, the claim that someone could have been greater than they actually are will be represented as the claim that there is some possible world in which that individual is greater than that individual is in the actual world. While I will as much as possible remain neutral on metaphysical questions about the nature of possible worlds, one useful way to think of possible worlds is as certain sorts of properties which the universe could have, but does not, instantiate. On this construal, the idea that there are possible worlds—properties that the universe could have had, but doesn't—is just a special case of the fact that there are properties which things could have had, but in fact lack.

So when we are stating claims about the relative greatness of certain individuals, it is best to think of these as comparing the relative greatness of certain individual/world pairs. In what follows I will use

$x_w$

to mean

$x$ in world $w$

As is standard, I will use '$\alpha$' to represent the actual world. So

$$x_\alpha$$

will mean

$x$ in the actual world

and

$$x_w > y_{w^*}$$

expresses the transworld comparative claim that $x$ is, in $w$, greater than $y$ is in $w^*$.[16]

These world-indicating subscripts are required to make sense of reasoning from the claim that God is the greatest possible, as well as the greatest actual, being. But an additional complication is required to mark the distinction between the claim that God is the greatest possible and the greatest conceivable being.

As we'll see in Chapter 3, there are many different senses in which a being might be said to be conceivable. But, as a first pass, we can say that a being is conceivable iff it is conceivable, or imaginable, that that being exists, and that a claim is conceivable if it can be conceived, or imagined, to be true. Just as the apparatus of possible worlds is useful to model claims about the greatness of beings which could have but do not exist, so we can introduce conceivable worlds to model claims about the greatness of beings which can be imagined to exist, but in fact do not. Just as possible worlds may be thought of as properties which the universe could have had but lacks, conceivable worlds may be thought of as properties which the universe could be imagined to have, but in fact lacks.

It is now widely held that some claims are conceivable—can be, in some sense, imagined or conceived to be true—but are not genuinely possible. If this is correct, then there are some conceivable worlds

---

[16] Here and in what follows I will write as though $>$ is a strict total order on actual and possible things. That is not a mandatory assumption for the perfect being theologian; she could hold that some things are incommensurable. I set this possibility aside for simplicity; nothing in the arguments to follow hangs on it.

which are not possible worlds. I will be assuming that this is correct. The point of this assumption at this stage is to give the perfect being theologian maximum flexibility. For if the possible worlds just are the conceivable worlds, then the claims that God is the greatest possible being and that God is the greatest conceivable being are equivalent. At this stage we want to leave open the possibility that the distinction between possibility and conceivability might do some genuine work in helping us to derive the properties of God. Much as we represented possible worlds with '$w$' subscripts, we can represent conceivable worlds with '$c$' subscripts.

This gives us the resources to formulate our three modal principles, perspicuously if anachronistically, as

$$[G\alpha B][\forall x: x \neq God] (God_\alpha > x_\alpha)$$
$$[GPB][\forall x: x \neq God] \forall w \in W (God_\alpha > x_w)$$
$$[GCB][\forall x: x \neq God] \forall c \in C (God_\alpha > x_c)$$

where $W$ is the set of all possible worlds and $C$ is the set of all conceivable worlds. Each principle entails the claims above it, given that all possible worlds are conceivable—and hence that $W \subseteq C$—and that the actual world is possible—and hence that $\alpha \in W$.[17]

It is worth noting that each of these modal principles immediately implies that God exists, since each attributes a relational property to God. This makes these formulations highly unsuitable for some uses to which the claim that God is the greatest (actual, possible, or conceivable) being is sometimes put. An important example is the case of debates between theists and atheists about the existence of God, in which the principle that God is the greatest possible being might function as a kind of regulative principle, one which is used to define the type of being whose existence is in dispute.[18] In these contexts, the

---

[17] In what follows, I'll often simplify the formal notation by omitting the quantification over worlds—unbound subscripts should always be understood as bound by universal quantifiers with wide scope. Here and in what follows I set aside any scruples about possibilist quantification, and simply help myself to it. While this is something to which one might reasonably object in other contexts, here it is a gift to the perfect being theologian. If the relevant claims cannot be reformulated without loss in a more ontologically conservative way, then this would be a further problem for the project.

[18] For an extended use of this strategy, see van Inwagen (2006).

claim that God is the greatest possible being is better formulated as a biconditional than as predicating something of God. I'll return to this topic in Chapter 6 below. But as in the next few chapters our focus will be on the attempt to derive the properties of God, while taking the existence of God for granted, it will be simpler to stick with the formulations above.

I will, for obvious reasons, call perfect being theologies based on [GαB] or [GPB] *alethic* perfect being theologies, and those based on [GCB] *epistemic* perfect being theologies.

## 1.5 Greatness conditions

This notation also gives us the resources to formulate greatness conditions. Greatness conditions are conditions which properties can satisfy or not, and it is simplest to formulate them as schemata which involve a single predicate letter. Consider, for example, the condition a property satisfies iff, necessarily, everything which has the property is greater than everything which lacks it. That can be expressed using the schema:

$$\forall x \forall y \left( (Fx_w \ \& \ \neg Fy_{w*}) \rightarrow x_w > y_{w*} \right)$$

A property meets this condition just in case replacing '$F$' with a predicate expressing that property results in a true formula.

Before going any further, it's worth considering an important objection to the way that I have set things up. Advocates of divine simplicity may be inclined to object to the way that I suggest formulating greatness conditions, on the grounds that talk of the properties of God is somehow misconceived—however we understand divine attribute talk, according to this sort of view, it shouldn't be understood in any way metaphysically serious enough to entail God's metaphysical complexity.[19]

This worry is fair enough. But it seems to me that it is basically orthogonal to the sort of project under discussion. For even advocates

---

[19] Thanks to Mike Rea for pointing this out.

of divine simplicity think that there is some distinction between predications like 'God is omnipotent,' on the one hand, and 'God is powerless,' on the other. The former are correct in some way that the latter are not—if this were not so, it's hard to see how advocates of divine simplicity like Aquinas could consistently spend so much time discussing questions about the divine attributes.

But whether this 'correctness' is cashed out in terms of literal truth, or in terms of some theory of analogical predication, or in some other way, is beside the present point. For we can recast the above formulation of greatness conditions in terms of predicates and correctness (in whatever the favored sense of this term is), without making any mention of properties. In these terms, we can say that a predicate $\phi$ meets the above greatness condition just in case replacing '$F$' with $\phi$ yields a formula which is, in the theorist's chosen sense, correct.

In what follows, I'll for convenience help myself to the more metaphysically heavy-duty talk of properties. But it is worth bearing in mind that this is just a convenience, and could all be recast in terms of predicates and some less committal understanding of the correctness of certain divine predications.

*   *   *

The purest sort of perfect being theology would consist of one of our three modal principles, plus a greatness condition which satisfies our desiderata. The next two chapters argue that there is no successful pure version of perfect being theology. (Chapter 2 is devoted to alethic perfect being theologies; Chapter 3 to epistemic perfect being theologies.) This is a surprising result. But it is not quite the disaster it may seem. While perfect being theology is often presented as fitting this mold, the way that some advocates of perfect being theology actually proceed suggests a slightly more complex model—one which requires more substantial assumptions about God than any of our three modal principles. I'll turn to these impure versions of perfect being theology in Chapter 4 below.

# 2

# Alethic Perfect Being Theology

In the previous chapter, we considered three different modal principles which might serve as the starting point for a perfect being theology: the claims that God is the greatest actual being, that God is the greatest possible being, and that God is the greatest conceivable being. Our next question is: is there any way to argue from any of these principles, plus a greatness condition, to the properties of God in a way which meets the desiderata sketched above?

## 2.1 The greatest actual being

While, in practice, contemporary perfect being theologians invariably rely on a modal principle stronger than the claim that God is the greatest actual being, it is instructive to begin by adopting [GαB] as our modal principle. As we'll see, the problems we encounter here will recur in different forms when we strengthen the modal principle to obtain more familiar forms of 'perfect being' reasoning.

Recall that the principle that God is the greatest actual being can be formulated as follows:

[GαB]   $[\forall x: x \neq \text{God}] (\text{God}_\alpha > x_\alpha)$

What greatness condition can be usefully paired with this principle to derive claims about the attributes of God? A natural choice is the following:

[α1]   $\forall x \forall y ((Fx_\alpha \& \neg Fy_\alpha) \to x_\alpha > y_\alpha)$

A property satisfies this condition just in case everything which actually has it is greater than everything which actually lacks it. It seems reasonably plausible, at first glance, that every property which meets this condition would be a property of the greatest actual being.

But this would be a mistake. Consider the following parallel inference: Sally is the smartest student in the class; anyone with an I.Q. over 400 is smarter than anyone with an I.Q. below 400; therefore, Sally has an I.Q. over 400. The argument is invalid without the extra premise that someone in the class has an I.Q. over 400.

Just so, the argument that any property satisfying [$\alpha$1] would be a property of the greatest actual being is invalid without the extra premise that the candidate divine attribute is instantiated. So [$\alpha$1] fails the [Entailment] requirement, since a property, e.g. the property of being a flying pig, can satisfy it without being a property of the greatest actual being. And the fact that it fails [Entailment] is of course a very good thing for the perfect being theologian, since, if [$\alpha$1] did satisfy [Entailment], the fact that every uninstantiated property satisfies [$\alpha$1] would be a reductio of [G$\alpha$B] (along with our stronger modal principles).

It might seem pretty easy to fix this problem; and in a way it is. We can build into our schema the requirement that the property in question be instantiated:

$$[\alpha 2] \quad \exists x F x_\alpha \ \& \ \forall x \forall y \left( (F x_\alpha \ \& \ \neg F y_\alpha) \rightarrow x_\alpha > y_\alpha \right)$$

This is not satisfied by the property of being a flying pig, which is good. And, more generally, this principle does meet the [Entailment] condition—any property which meets it must be a property of the greatest actual being. For suppose that a property meets it. Then it must (by the first conjunct) be instantiated by some being—call it Bob. Suppose for reductio that the property is not instantiated by the greatest actual being. Then, by the second conjunct of the greatness condition, Bob would be greater than the greatest actual being, which is a contradiction.

The problem with this greatness condition is not that it fails [Entailment] but rather that it scores very poorly with [Informativeness]. For suppose that we want to derive the result that God is omnipotenⱼ To do that, we have to first ask whether omnipotence satisfies this greatness condition; and to answer this question, we have to know whether omnipotence is actually instantiated. The obvious problem is that, given that it seems quite implausible that something other than God is omnipotent, it seems that we have to know whether God is omnipotent in order to know whether omnipotence satisfies $[\alpha 2]$. We seem to be spinning our wheels.

The problem recurs for many of the traditional candidates for the divine attributes. In the case of omniscience, perfect goodness, and creation of the universe, as with omnipotence, it is hard to see how we could figure out whether these properties are instantiated—and hence whether they satisfy the first conjunct of the proposed greatness condition—without first knowing whether they are instantiated by God.[1]

Now, this does not mean that the present line of argument does not get us *anything*. For suppose that Michael Jordan is the greatest entity with which we are acquainted. Then we are entitled to conclude from the conjunction of $[G\alpha B]$ and $[\alpha 2]$ that God is at least as great as Michael Jordan. But this is a pretty unimpressive result. (Note that we are not even licensed to assume that, for example, God has as much knowledge as the most knowledgeable thing with which we are acquainted; there is no guarantee that there is an actual being which both possesses that knowledge and has at least as much overall greatness as the greatest being with which we are acquainted.)

It is very natural to respond to this problem by strengthening one's modal principle. For surely, even if it is sometimes difficult to know whether, for example, omnipotence is instantiated without first knowing whether God is omnipotent, we can know whether it is

---

[1] Other traditional candidates for divine attributes produce slightly different, but related, failures of [Informativeness]. For example, eternity and immateriality seem not to meet this condition, since some non-eternal and material things —like you and I—seem to be greater than some eternal and immaterial things—like the number 4. More on this sort of problem in §2.2 below.

ceivable, that omnipotence be instantiated without
of the divine attributes.

## 2.2 The greatest possible being

So let's turn instead to the principle that God is the greatest possible
being:

[GPB]  $[\forall x: x \neq \text{God}] \, \forall w \in W \, (\text{God}_\alpha > x_w)$

It might seem, at first, pretty easy to formulate a greatness condition to
pair with [GPB]. For if, necessarily, it is better for anything to be $F$ than
not-$F$, this fact seems like it, in conjunction with [GPB], should entail
that God is $F$. This might suggest the following greatness condition:

[P1]  $\forall x \forall y \, ((Fx_w \, \& \, \neg Fy_{w*}) \rightarrow x_w > y_{w*})$

A property satisfies this condition just in case it is impossible for a
thing which lacks the property to be better than a thing which has it.

But a moment's inspection shows that this runs into problems
closely related to those which faced [$\alpha$1]. Vacuously, any property
which is necessarily uninstantiated will satisfy this schema—but we
obviously don't want properties like the property of being nonexistent,
or the property of having proved that $2 + 2 = 5$, to be among the divine
attributes. And, just as it does not follow from the fact that a property
satisfies [$\alpha$1] that it is a property of the greatest actual being, it does
not follow from the fact that these properties satisfy [P1] that they are
properties of the greatest possible being. So [P1] fails [Entailment].
(And, as above, this is a very good thing for the perfect theologian,
since otherwise the fact that the property of having proved that
$2 + 2 = 5$ satisfies [P1] would be a reductio of our modal principle.)

But there's an easy fix available. To surmount this problem—unlike
the problem with [$\alpha$1] and [G$\alpha$B]—we don't need to require that the
property be instantiated; it is enough to require that it be possibly
instantiated:

[P2]  (i) $\Diamond \exists x Fx$ & (ii) $\forall x \forall y \, ((Fx_w \, \& \, \neg Fy_{w*}) \rightarrow x_w > y_{w*})$

A property meets this condition just in case it meets both of the following conditions: (i) possibly, something has it; and (ii) anything in any world with the property is greater than anything in any world which lacks it.

While [P2] is an improvement over [P1], it isn't a satisfactory stopping point. This is because [P2] seems to fail [Informativeness]. This is because, it seems, for any property we can imagine a pair of beings such that the one without it is greater than the one with it.

For suppose that we are wondering whether immateriality satisfies the above condition. One might argue that it does not, by pointing out that Barack Obama, a material thing, is greater than the number 4, an immaterial thing. This is sufficient to show that immateriality does not satisfy [P2]—but is hardly the sort of argument which should call into question the status of immateriality as a divine attribute![2]

The same sort of argument, it seems, could be used to show that any candidate attribute fails to satisfy [P2]. Consider omniscience. It seems reasonably clear that an omnipotent being with almost perfect knowledge would be greater than an omniscient but relatively powerless being. But, if that is right, omniscience fails to satisfy [P2]. Just so, it is plausible that an omniscient and perfectly good being which lacks a few trivial powers would be greater than an omnipotent being which lacked goodness and knowledge. Parallel remarks apply to other traditional candidates for the divine attributes.

One could of course reply at this stage by saying that God is necessarily omnipotent, omniscient, and perfectly good and that, since it is impossible for there to be more than one omnipotent being in a world, it is impossible for there to be an omnipotent being which lacked goodness and knowledge. But this would of course be to import (very) substantial assumptions about God in our attempt to see whether a given property satisfies our greatness condition—which we can

---

[2] If, bizarrely, you think that numbers are greater than people, this would not avoid the problem—for then the example would entail that freedom and personhood, which Obama has but number 4 lacks, fail to satisfy the condition.

hardly do if we aim to use that greatness condition to learn about the properties of God.[3]

The moral of these examples is that for any candidate divine attribute, we can imagine a situation in which a being with that attribute is less great than a being without it, simply by imagining the latter to have other properties which outweigh the attribute in question. Call this the problem of *trumping*. As we will see, this is a central problem for the attempt to formulate an alethic perfect being theology, and different versions of alethic perfect being theology can largely be classified based on how they respond to it.

The problem of trumping is not new. Indeed, Anselm saw clearly that this sort of problem arises for the attempt to derive the divine attributes from the claim that God is the greatest possible being. In the *Monologion* (§15) he points out that

one who is just, but not wise, is apparently a better man than one who is wise, but not just

which is just to say, in our terms, that wisdom can be trumped— despite the fact that we want to count wisdom among the divine attributes. The ubiquity of the problem of trumping suggests that [P2] fails the [Informativeness] condition.

In the next two sections I'll discuss what I see as the two most promising strategies for the alethic perfect being theologian to solve the problem of trumping.

## 2.3 The restriction strategy

The problem of trumping, one might think, brings out a fairly obvious sense in which [P2] (like [P1], and our two $\alpha$-schemata) is too simple. The key seems to be that the above schemata do not require that the values of $x, y$ that we compare for greatness be at all similar. And, as the examples used to illustrate the problem of trumping show, this

---

[3] I will, however, return to a related strategy, which relies on grouping various attributes together, in §2.4 below.

seems to be something that we clearly should require. The fact that Barack Obama is greater than the number 4 does not speak to the credentials of the property of immateriality just because Obama's relative greatness is explained by attributes other than immateriality— like consciousness and freedom—with respect to which Obama and the number differ.

It is natural, given this, to restrict the pairs of entities comparison of which can be used to decide whether some candidate divine attribute satisfies our greatness condition. Let's call this reply to the problem of trumping the *restriction strategy*.

The restriction strategy seems to be at least part of Anselm's solution to the problem of trumping; in the passage immediately following the one quoted above, he writes

yet, taken by itself, it is not better not to be wise than to be wise. For, everything that is not wise, simply in so far as it is not wise, is less than what is wise, since everything that is not wise would be better if it were wise.

The meaning of 'simply in so far as it is not wise' seems to be something like 'holding fixed all properties other than the lack of wisdom.' One might think, then, that our greatness condition should restrict quantification to pairs of individuals who are the same with respect to all properties other than $F$.

While a plausible first step, this can't be quite right. The reason is that in the case of most properties it is impossible for there to be a pair of individuals which differ *only* with respect to that property. Consider, for example, the property of knowing that $2 + 2 = 4$. Two subjects couldn't differ only with respect to possession of that property, since presumably which propositions a subject knows supervenes on other aspects of that subject's mental life—two subjects could not both believe that $2 + 2 = 4$, and be alike with respect to all epistemic properties of that belief, and still differ in that one knows the proposition and the other does not.

So some refining is in order, and what seems to be wanted is something like this: $x$, $y$ are a relevant pair iff one is $F$ and the other is not, and the two are as similar as it is possible for two things which differ with respect to $F$-ness to be.[4] Call a pair of entities which satisfy this condition $F$-duplicates. This gives us:

[P3]   $\Diamond \exists x F x$ & $\forall x \forall y$ (($Fx_w$ & $\neg Fy_{w*}$ & $< x_w, y_{w*} >$ are $F$-duplicates) $\rightarrow x_w > y_{w*}$)

This is just like [P2], but for the restriction of entities whose greatness is to be compared to $F$-duplicates.

But this natural proposal runs into a serious problem: the problem of essentially better-making properties. The problem is that there are properties which are such that anything with the property is greater than the most similar possible thing without it—but still, for all that, not plausible candidates to be divine attributes.

Consider a healthy earthworm which instantiates the property of having a well-functioning circulatory system. It is plausible that if we compare any two beings alike except for the fact that one has this property and one lacks it, the former will be greater than the latter. This is because having a well-functioning circulatory system entails the possession of other properties, like having a circulatory system, having a body, etc. Hence if we compare any two beings alike except that one has a well-functioning circulatory systems, we will always be comparing a pair of beings with circulatory systems, with bodies, and in general alike except for the fact that one's circulatory system is, and the other's is not, functioning properly. Surely in such a case the former will always be greater than the latter. Hence having a well-functioning circulatory system satisfies [P3]. But, for all that, we don't think that God has a circulatory system, whether well-functioning or not.

The problem is that properties like having a well-functioning circulatory system satisfy the following three conditions:

(i) they are possibly instantiated, and hence satisfy the first conjunct of [P3];

---

[4] This is roughly the definition of 'great-making properties' given in Hill (2004), 9.

(ii) they are such that any two beings which are as similar as it is possible to be given that the first has the property and the second lacks it are such that the first is greater than the second, and hence satisfy the second conjunct of [P3];
(iii) but they are not plausible candidates to be divine attributes.

Other instances of the problem, which also plausibly satisfy (i)–(iii), include the property of being a well-mixed martini, the property of being perfectly functioning dishwasher—you get the idea.

This is not unrelated to another problem which Anselm noticed. In the *Monologion* he points out that

in some cases, not to be a certain thing is better than to be it, as not to be gold may be better than to be gold. For it is better for man not to be gold, than to be gold; although it might be better for something to be gold, than not to be gold—lead, for instance. For though both, namely, man and lead are not gold, man is something as much better than gold, as he would be of inferior nature, were he gold; while lead is something as much more base than gold, as it would be more precious, were it gold.[5]

Part of Anselm's point is that which properties it is better to have than lack—even holding fixed the entity's other properties—can depend on what kind of thing the entity in question is. The result is that a property can be better to have than lack for all members of some kinds without being the sort of property which would be better to have than lack for members of other kinds. The present objection is just that this point, together with the additional claim that some such properties are better to have than lack for all things capable of having them, makes trouble for [P3].

This would be extremely bad news if [P3] satisfied the [Entailment] condition, since then we would have in effect falsified the claim

---

[5] It is not completely clear from *Monologion* §15 what Anselm's reply to this problem is. One reasonable interpretation, defended in Leftow (2004), is that Anselm restricts attention to those properties which would be better to have than lack for members of the highest kind of being, which is the kind 'deity'. If so, then Anselm can be thought of as endorsing something like the greatness condition [P5], discussed below.

that God is the greatest possible being. But in fact [P3] fails the [Entailment] condition. If a property $F$ satisfies [P3], then we know that, of every possible pair of $F$-duplicates—that is, every pair of things such that one is $F$ and the other is as much like the first thing as a non-$F$ thing can be—the one which is $F$ is greater. But that only entails that God is $F$ if it is possible that God be one of a pair of $F$-duplicates. And in the cases just discussed, this extra assumption is false.

I now want to consider two responses to the problem of essentially better-making properties for the restriction strategy. The first simply extends the restriction strategy further, by further restricting the pairs of entities which we can use to test whether some property satisfies our condition. The second adds a restriction on admissible properties, which rules out properties like having a well-functioning circulatory system from the start.

### 2.3.1 The extended restriction strategy

One natural thought is that the problem posed by the example of the earthworm arises from the fact that we are looking at the wrong entities. Who cares, one might think, whether an earthworm would be better than its twin with a slightly less well-functioning nervous system? The case is so far distant from the question of the divine attributes that it may seem unsurprising that any test for divine attributes which gives earthworms a role to play goes wrong.

It is natural to implement this idea by further restricting the quantification over entities to beings which are more relevant to questions about the divine attributes than are earthworms. So, for example, we could restrict consideration to persons. Then our greatness condition would look like this:

[P4]   $\Diamond \exists x F x$ & $\forall x \forall y ((F x_w$ & $\neg F y_{w*}$ & $x_w, y_{w*}$ are persons & $< x_w, y_{w*} >$ are $F$-duplicates) $\rightarrow x_w > y_{w*})$

But it is not hard to see that this does not really help with the problem of essentially beneficial properties. Human beings are persons, and some of them have well-functioning nervous systems. Since God is not a possible $F$-duplicate of a human being with a well-functioning nervous system, [P4] fails [Entailment] for basically the same reason as [P3]. If restricting the range of our quantifiers is going to help, we need to do some more restricting.

But it is hard to know what restriction to try next. Perhaps we could restrict our attention to immaterial persons. But this would face two problems. The first is simply that we would be building into our test the assumption that God is immaterial and a person—two claims about God we might wish to derive rather than stipulate.

The second, much more serious, problem is a kind of dilemma. Either there are possible immaterial persons other than God—say, angels—or there are not. If there are, then it is plausible that the problem of essentially beneficial properties will resurface. For presumably there is some property $F$ which is such that every angel with the property is better than its $F$-duplicate. But this should not entail that God is $F$, for the property might well be one which beings limited in the way that angels are limited can have—much as the property of having a well-functioning nervous system is one that only material beings can have. In this case it will not be possible for God to be an $F$-duplicate of an angel, and our revised test will fail [Entailment].

So suppose instead that there are not possible immaterial persons other than God. Then the restriction of our relevant pairs will be equivalent to a restriction to possible states of God. This would yield the following greatness condition:

$$\Diamond \exists x F x \ \& \ ((F(\text{God})_w \ \& \ \neg F(\text{God})_{w*} \ \& \ <\text{God}_w, \text{God}_{w*} > \text{ are } F\text{-duplicates}) \rightarrow \text{God}_w > \text{God}_{w*})$$

But this won't do. Consider any property which is possibly instantiated, but not instantiated by God—like the property of having a circulatory system. This property will satisfy the first part of this condition and vacuously satisfy the second. This is exactly the opposite of what we want—and shows that this condition fails to satisfy [Entailment].[6]

---

[6] The same criticism could have been made of [P4]—I skipped it above for simplicity, since that condition can be seen to be unsatisfactory on other grounds.

Fortunately, the needed modification is, it might seem, pretty obvious:

[P5]   $\Diamond$(God is $F$) & (($F(\text{God})_w$ & $\neg F(\text{God})_{w*}$ & $<\text{God}_w,$ $\text{God}_{w*}>$ are $F$-duplicates) $\rightarrow$ $\text{God}_w > \text{God}_{w*}$)

A property satisfies this condition, intuitively, just in case possibly, God has it, and all else being equal, God is greater with the property than without it. This satisfies [Entailment], and would seem to avoid the problem of better-making properties, since the problematic properties discussed above will not satisfy the first conjunct of [P5].

Though fitting him into the model of a pure alethic perfect being theology oversimplifies his view,[7] this has some similarities to the sort of greatness condition envisaged by Brian Leftow in *God and Necessity*. In an admirably explicit statement of his method, he writes:

Nothing could be a better G . . . than God in fact is. God can be F. God would be a better G were he F than were he not F . . . Suppose now for reductio that God is not F. Then God is not as good a G as He could be. So if God is not F, it is false that nothing could be a better G than God in fact is. But this is true. So, *prima facie*, God is F.[8]

Here Leftow seems to be comparing the following two hypotheses: that God is $F$, and that God is not-$F$. He then proposes that we ask which hypothesis makes God greater and, on the basis of the claim that God is the greatest possible being, concludes that that hypothesis is true. That is, he seems to be reasoning from [P5], plus [GPB], to claims about the divine attributes.

This is an important break from all of the greatness conditions sketched above—all of those focused on the relative greatness of arbitrary beings, rather than hypotheses specifically about God.[9]

---

[7] In the end, he is better understood as advocating what in Chapter 4 I call an 'impure perfect being theology.' See §4.2 for discussion of Leftow's more nuanced views.

[8] Leftow (2012), 9–10. I discuss the reason for the '*prima facie*' qualification in Chapter 5 below.

[9] It contrasts with, e.g., the method of Hoffman and Rosenkrantz (2008), §1.2, who compare God with other members of the general kind 'Entity.' More on their view in §4.2 below.

And [P5] seems, for that reason, to avoid at least some of the problems which they face. Though writers are often not explicit about exactly how the derivation of the divine attributes is supposed to work, at least many write in such a way as to suggest that they have something like [P5] in mind.

Unfortunately, [P5] faces what seems to me to be a decisive objection. The problem, somewhat ironically, derives from the method of perfect being theology itself. Advocates of perfect being theology often argue, plausibly, that for any property which it is intrinsically good to have, it is better to have that property necessarily rather than merely contingently.[10] As Hoffman & Rosenkrantz say,

... to say that a being is *incorruptible* is to say that it has its perfections *necessarily*... Evidently, all other things being equal, such a being is greater than one which... could fail to have one or more of its perfections.[11]

Given this line of thought, it seems plausible that God is not just the greatest possible being, but also necessarily the greatest possible being.[12] So it seems that the advocate of [GPB] should also endorse its necessitation:

$$[\forall x: x \neq \text{God}] \; \forall w, w^* \in W \; (\text{God}_{w^*} > x_w)$$

But this does not quite express the claim that God is necessarily the greatest possible being. What it says is that God is necessarily greater than all things other than God. But it leaves open the possibility that God is, in some world, less great than God is in another world. And

---

[10] One might find initially attractive the stronger and simpler claim that, for any property which it is better to have than lack, it is better to have that property essentially than accidentally. But some properties are only better to have than to lack due to contingent features of one's environment—e.g., the property of being well-adapted to the climate of the earth—and there is presumably no special good in having those properties essentially rather than accidentally. Thanks to Dustin Crummett for pointing this out. See Chapter 4 for more on the distinction between intrinsic and extrinsic goods.

[11] Hoffman and Rosenkrantz (2008), 18–19.

[12] Though there are complexities here, which I set to the side, involving the question of whether God can be greater at one time than another. While this would be denied by most perfect being theologians, it would be accepted by some process theologians (e.g. Hartshorne (1962)), many of whom would wish to endorse some version of the claim that God is the greatest possible being.

this is a possibility that the perfect being theologian should want to rule out, for surely it would be greater for God to be essentially such that *nothing* in any world is greater than God is in this world. That claim may be expressed as follows:

[□GPB]   $\forall x \forall w, w^* \in W \neg (x_w > \text{God}_{w^*})$

So let's assume that the proponent of an alethic perfect being theology will accept [□GPB]. The problem is that, if [□GPB] is true, then so is the following:

$\forall w \forall w^* \neg (\text{God}_w > \text{God}_{w^*})$

But this poses a very serious problem for our greatness condition, [P5]. For suppose that we argue successfully that it is better for God to be $F$ than not $F$. It does not yet follow that $F$ satisfies [P5]; for that, we need to also know that God is possibly $F$.

But we already know from [□GPB] that God is necessarily $F$ or necessarily not $F$. And, given this, the claim that God is possibly $F$ is trivially equivalent to the conclusion—that God is $F$—for which we wished to argue. This means that, to see whether some candidate property satisfies the first conjunct of [P5], we already need to know something which is trivially equivalent to the claim that that property is a property of God. Hence [P5] can never yield the result that a given property is among the divine attributes without being given as input something trivially equivalent to just that.

Let's call this the *problem of triviality*. The problem of triviality shows that [P5] fails our [Informativeness] desideratum in an especially dramatic way, for we can derive nothing from [P5] about God that we do not already bring to our inquiry.

It may be worth looking at a concrete example of a 'perfect being argument' which makes use of [GPB] and something like [P5], to see how these abstract considerations come to the surface in a particular instance of 'perfect being' reasoning. Let's look at Leftow's argument that God is responsible for the 'truth-explainers' for all necessary truths, which he labels 'NEC':

NEC. $(P)(\Box P$ is true $\rightarrow$ God is, contains, has, has attributes that have (etc.) or produces all its truth-explainers)[13]

Leftow explains in some depth both what he means by a 'truth-explainer' and the reasons behind the 'is, contains, has, etc.' qualification—for our purposes, we can abstract from these details and turn directly to his argument in favor of NEC, which looks to be an attempt to argue from something like [P5] to a conclusion about God:

It would be an awesome thing to be unconstrained even by modal truths and facts of modal status . . . A being whose power is not externally limited even by these would seem more powerful than one whose power was subject to such a constraint. (NEC) secures this awesome lack of constraint. So if (NEC) is viable, theists have 'perfect-being' reason to accept it.[14]

To put the argument in the terms introduced above, let's use $w^{NEC}$ as a name for a world in which NEC is true, and $w^{\neg NEC}$ as a name for a world in which NEC is false. Then Leftow's central claim may be put like this:

$$\text{God}_{w^{NEC}} > \text{God}_{w^{\neg NEC}}$$

This says, roughly, that God would be greater in a world in which God explained all of the necessary truths than in a world in which God does not. For the reasons that Leftow gives, this claim is not without plausibility.

The key question, though, is not whether this claim is true, but whether, as Leftow seems to think, it follows from this claim together with [GPB] that NEC is true. The problem is that this does not follow without the help of an extra assumption:

NEC is possible.

For suppose that this assumption is false, and that NEC is not possibly true. Then the hypothesis that NEC is false, even given the truth of Leftow's comparative greatness claim, would not contradict [GPB].

---

[13] Leftow (2012), 115.    [14] Leftow (2012), 134.

That principle, after all, only says that God is the greatest *possible* being; it says nothing about how God's greatness compares with the greatness of beings in various impossible situations.

It is tempting to simply add to Leftow's argument the assumption that NEC is possible. And, looking at the above quote from Leftow, it might seem that it was his intention to include the possibility of NEC as a premise; that, presumably, is why his description of the argument for NEC includes the assumption that 'NEC is viable.' But the problem with this move, of course, is that if [□GPB] is true, then (given the truth of Leftow's claim about comparative greatness) NEC and its negation are both necessary if possible. Given this, the additional possibility assumption is—given that possible necessity is equivalent to necessity—equivalent to the conclusion to be argued for. So the assumption that NEC is possible, while needed to make the derivation of the attribute valid, also obviates the need for that derivation. If we knew that NEC was possible, we wouldn't have to appeal to the greatness of God's explaining the necessary truths to derive its truth. The claim that God is the greatest possible being is here an idle wheel. This is the problem of triviality.

One might reply that, even if considerations of greatness can't do all the work here, and need to be supplemented with the claim that the relevant hypothesis about God is possible, that doesn't mean that 'perfect being' reasoning is doing no work; after all, that reasoning is what got us to the claim that the relevant hypothesis is necessary if possible, which is surely not a trivial one.[15]

While the basic point here is correct, it does not do much to help the alethic perfect being theologian. One way to see this is to note that if we started, not with the assumption that NEC is possible, but instead with the contrary premise that

¬NEC is possible.

---

[15] This is the reply suggested by Leftow (2015), which is a response to an earlier version of the present argument given in Speaks (2014).

it would follow from this, together with Leftow's claim about comparative greatness and [□GPB], that NEC is false. In general, if we have a pair of claims $p$, $q$, and God would be greater if $p$ than if $q$, the possibility of *either* $p$ or $q$ would suffice for its truth—it matters not at all which of them would make God greater, since any asymmetry of greatness is sufficient to make both necessary, and hence true, if possible. Given this, it is hard to see how alethic perfect being reasoning could even slightly increase our credence in a hypothesis like NEC—it gives us the result that both NEC and its negation are necessary if possible, but no clue as to which is possible.

Imagine, for comparison, a mathematician wondering whether Goldbach's conjecture or its negation is true. It will not help her to be told that both the conjecture and its negation are, if possible, necessary. Indeed, this new information is unlikely to cause her to adjust her credence in the conjecture. Just so, I think, even if we accept the claim that God is necessarily the greatest possible being and the claim that God would be greater with the relevant property than without it, these give us no reason to raise our credence at all in the relevant claim about God. This sort of perfect being reasoning does not move the needle.

This is not, of course, to deny that arguments for the claim that a given proposition is necessary if possible are sometimes of philosophical significance. For example, Kripke's defense of the Cartesian premise that if it is possible that mind and body be distinct, then they necessarily are, is of great philosophical significance. But that is because it comes packaged with a plausible conceivability argument for the relevant possibility claim. In the present case, we have no such thing.

The problem here has nothing to do with the special case of the relationship between God and modal truths, and everything to do with the greatness condition with which we are working. The problem is that if [□GPB] is true, then no property satisfies all of the following conditions:

Possibly, God is $F$
Possibly, God is not $F$
It is better for God to be $F$ than not $F$

But such a property is just what we would need for the second conjunct of [P5] to be non-vacuously satisfied.

It is natural to respond to this problem by noting that, even if we never have a pair of possible hypotheses about God of the right sort, such a pair of hypotheses might nonetheless be conceivable. And perhaps this fact, plus the claim that God is the greatest conceivable being, might get us the results we want. This is a promising strategy; but it is to abandon alethic perfect being theology in favor of an epistemic perfect being theology. I return to this strategy in Chapter 3 below.

### 2.3.2 Pure vs. impure perfections

Let's turn instead to a different approach. Our first response to the problem of trumping was the restriction strategy, which restricts relevant entities to those which are maximally similar. This, in turn, led to the problem of essentially better-making properties, like the property of having a well-functioning circulatory system, which satisfy [P3] but are not plausible candidates to be divine attributes. Above we considered further restrictions on the relevant entities, which culminated with a restriction to possible states of God, and the problem of triviality. A different response to the problem of essentially better-making properties, though, would be, not to further restrict the relevant individuals, but rather to make restrictions on the class of eligible properties.

One appealing way to do this begins with a distinction drawn by Scotus, between pure and mixed perfections. A pure perfection is one which 'includes no limitation in itself' and so 'does not necessarily include some concomitant imperfection.' A mixed perfection, by contrast, 'includes some limitation and therefore necessarily has some added imperfection.'[16] Scotus thought, reasonably enough, that only pure perfections could be predicated of God.

---

[16] Scotus (1987), 94.

Following Scotus,[17] then, we might then modify [P3] to add a condition requiring that the relevant property be a pure perfection, as follows:

[P6]  $\Diamond \exists x F x$  & $F$ is a pure perfection & $\forall x \forall y$  (($Fx_w$ & $\neg Fy_{w*}$ & $< x_w, y_{w*} >$ are $F$-duplicates) $\rightarrow x_w > y_{w*}$)

This would seem to be enough to avoid the problem of essentially better-making properties, since the property of having a well-functioning nervous system might well seem to be a mixed rather than a pure perfection. It entails materiality, after all, which might seem to be a limitation.

In the end, though, this simply leads to the problem of triviality via another route. For what does it mean for a property to be a pure perfection, in Scotus' sense? It is for that property not to include—which I take to mean 'entail'—a limitation. A limitation is presumably a property which limits—places an upper bound on—the greatness of a thing with that property. So it is a property which is such that anything with that property is less great than a thing could be. So it seems that a property is a pure perfection iff it satisfies the following schema:

$$\neg \exists G \forall x \forall w ((Fx_w \rightarrow Gx_w) \& (Gx_w \rightarrow \exists y \exists w^*(y_{w*} > x_w)))^{18}$$

A property $F$ satisfies this schema just in case there is no property which is such that (i) necessarily, every $F$-thing has it and (ii) necessarily, everything with the property is less great than some possible thing.

But then it is easy to see that satisfaction of the schema is extensionally equivalent to being a property of the greatest possible being. It is obvious that every property of the greatest possible being will

---

[17] While I say 'following Scotus,' I should add that it is very unclear whether Scotus thought that his distinction between pure and impure perfections could be put to use by the perfect being theologian. For an illuminating discussion, see Cross (2005), §3. I return to Cross' interpretation of Scotus' thoughts on perfect being theology below in §5.

[18] Obviously the quantification into predicate position here is dispensable.

satisfy this schema. To see the other direction, suppose that a property satisfies the schema. It follows that for every property which it entails, there is at least one being with the property than which there is no possible being which is greater. So every property which it entails—including itself—is a property of the greatest possible being.

Thus [P6] runs into exactly the same problem as [P5]. If we want to tell whether some property satisfies it, we first need to be able to tell whether it is a pure perfection. But to figure this out, we need to know whether it is a property of the greatest possible being. And that is just what we wanted our greatness condition to tell us. The problem of triviality (and not for the last time) simply resurfaces.

## 2.4  The conjunctive strategy

Let's take a step back. Early in the last section, we noticed a problem for [P2]: the fact that it permits comparison of quite disparate entities seems to stop it from satisfying [Informativeness], since, no matter how 'great-making' a property is, its positive effects can be swamped by the effects of other properties with respect to which the relevant pair of entities differ.

The response to this problem of trumping we explored in §2.3 was to restrict the relevant pairs of entities to maximally similar entities. While this was a natural response, it led us to a dead end. Our first attempt to implement the strategy led to the problem of essentially better-making properties, and the best solution to that problem turned out to be a restriction of relevant entities to possible states of God, which led to the problem of triviality. Restrictions on the class of admissible properties led to the same result.

It is time to try a different, more direct response to the problem of trumping. According to this response, our problems stem from the fact that we are considering properties 'one by one.' If we consider omniscience by itself, then, yes, it is plausible that it is possible for a non-omniscient being to be greater than an omniscient one. But suppose that we instead try out conjunctive properties, like the following:

$x$ is omniscient, omnipotent, and perfectly good.

When we consider conjunctive properties like this one, one might think, it is surely not so obvious that [P2] fails [Informativeness]. For if we imagine a being which is omniscient, omnipotent, and perfectly good, it is not so easy to imagine a greater being which lacks this property. And if the above property is possibly instantiated, and if we are licensed to conclude that there could be no greater being which lacks this property, we can conclude that the above property satisfies [P2]. And this, plus [GPB], implies that God possesses this conjunctive property, which gives us the desired result that God is omnipotent, omniscient, and perfectly good. Let's call this the *conjunctive strategy*.

To explore this strategy in more detail, let's think a bit more precisely about the conjunctive property the proponent of this strategy might begin with. Let us follow tradition and say that this conjunctive property should specify something about God's power, something about God's knowledge, and something about God's moral goodness. An initially plausible assumption about God's power might involve ascription of the following property:

[P]  for every state of affairs $s$ which it is possible for anything to bring about, $x$ can bring about $s$[19]

A natural starting point for describing God's knowledge would be the following property:

[K]  for every true proposition $p$, $x$ knows $p$

And, in the case of God's moral goodness:

[G]  in every situation, $x$ does the morally best thing which $x$ can do

The proponent of the conjunctive strategy can then propose the conjunctive property

---

[19]  This is a simplified version of analysis (B) in Flint and Freddoso (1983). Flint and Freddoso go on to complicate their analysis, in part to deal with the fact that, because it is impossible for someone to causally determine someone else to freely perform a certain action, states of affairs like 'Bob freely $\phi$s' can only be brought about by Bob—which would mean that nothing could instantiate [P]. Since this sort of case is orthogonal to my present interest, I set it aside for simplicity.

[Triple-O]: [P] & [K] & [G]

as a property which is both possibly instantiated and is such that, necessarily, anything with it is greater than anything without it. If so, then [Triple-O] will satisfy [P2], which is what we want.

But this does not quite solve the problem of trumping. Consider the question of whether it is greater to be perfectly good essentially, or merely accidentally. A reasonable case can be made that it is morally better to be essentially perfectly good than to have this trait accidentally. After all, it is a moral virtue to be such that one is not easily tempted to do the wrong thing; and it seems as though to possess this virtue in the highest degree would be to be such that it is *impossible* for one to do the wrong thing.[20] Let's use '[□G]' to stand for the property of having [G] essentially.

So far, this is no challenge to the claim that [Triple-O] satisfies [P2]. But it can be turned into one. Imagine a being which has the following conjunction of properties:

[P] & [□G] & knows everything besides a few insignificant propositions

Such a being will lack [K], and hence will not exemplify [Triple-O]. But surely a being with this property could be greater than a being which had [Triple-O], but lacked [□G]. For surely being so morally great as for it to be literally impossible for one to do the wrong thing is a more important trait than knowledge of a few insignificant propositions. So it seems that [Triple-O] does not satisfy [P2] after all.

The defender of the conjunctive strategy is unlikely to abandon all hope at this point. For she has an easy and natural solution: form a longer conjunction! We can simply add to our candidate conjunctive property the missing property which gave rise to the case of trumping. So consider, in this spirit, the following conjunctive property:

[P] & [K] & [□G]

---

[20] These are much the same intuitions used to argue for [□GPB] in §2.3.1 above. Recent presentations of this sort of argument for the conclusion that God is essentially perfectly good can be found in Morris (1985), §IV and Murray and Rea (2008), 21.

But parallel reasoning shows that this conjunctive property too can be trumped, and so also fails to satisfy [P2]. For consider the property [□P]—the property of being, not just omnipotent, but essentially so. Surely a being with this property could be greater than one with the former conjunctive property, for surely having the impressive property of being essentially omnipotent—of being such that it is literally impossible that one be less than all-powerful—can outweigh knowing a few insignificant propositions. So it looks like our previous property is trumped by

[□P] & [□G] & knows everything besides a few insignificant propositions

This suggests that the proponent of the conjunctive strategy should go with

[□P] & [K] & [□G]

But this too can be trumped. For consider [□E], the property of existing necessarily. This too is an impressive property; impressive enough, I suggest, that our conjunction is trumped by

[□P] & [□E] & [□G] & knows everything besides a few insignificant propositions

for surely the greatness of existing necessarily outweighs the imperfection of failing to know a few insignificant propositions. This suggests that the proponent of the conjunctive strategy should go with

[□P] & K & [□G] & [□E]

which brings us right to the doorstep of the familiar claim that the greatest possible being would exist necessarily, and be essentially omnipotent, omniscient, and perfectly good:

[□Triple-O]: [□P] & [□K] & [□G] & [□E]

A trumping argument can't take us over the threshold, since possession of [□K] entails possession of [K]. But for our purposes the difference between this last property and [□Triple-O] won't matter, so I'll assume that the proponent of the conjunctive strategy's best candidate for a property that satisfies [P2] is [□Triple-O].

Does this property satisfy [P2]? Let us concede for the purposes of argument that [□Triple-O] satisfies the second conjunct of [P2]: it is not the case that it is possible that some being without [□Triple-O] is greater than some being with it. That is to concede that [□Triple-O] is, as we might put it, 'greatest if possible': if [□Triple-O] is possibly instantiated, then [□Triple-O] is a property of the greatest possible being. Let's call properties of this sort, which satisfy the second conjunct of [P2], GIP-properties.

The question is then whether it satisfies the first conjunct—whether it is possibly instantiated. But of course—and here we get an echo of the problems that arose in connection with [P5]—if [□Triple-O] is possibly instantiated, then it is actually instantiated. And so the proponent of the conjunctive strategy faces something quite like the problem of triviality. To see whether [□Triple-O] satisfies [P2], we first need to know something trivially equivalent to the claim that [□Triple-O] is actually instantiated. And, while this is not immediately equivalent to the claim that [□Triple-O] is a property of God, it is very close indeed.

To get from the first claim to the second, after all, one need only assume the material conditional that if something is [□Triple-O], then God is—which is equivalent to the disjunction

Either it is not the case that some being is necessarily existent, and essentially omnipotent, omniscient, and perfectly morally good, or God is necessarily existent, and essentially omnipotent, omniscient, and perfectly morally good.

which is in turn equivalent to the claim that

Nothing which is not God has [□Triple-O].

This is an extraordinarily weak claim. It is one which an adherent of virtually any view of God—including one who denies that God has any of the traditional attributes—and virtually any sort of atheist would endorse. But given the truth of this very weak claim, it follows that [□Triple-O] is possibly instantiated iff it is a property of God. So, to be able to tell whether [□Triple-O] satisfies the first conjunct of our greatness condition, we have to know whether [□Triple-O] is one of the divine attributes. But that, of course, is the result that we wanted perfect being reasoning to deliver.

So far I have been presenting the problem for the conjunctive strategy as a close cousin of the problem of triviality. But the criticism can be presented in another way. Absent an independent argument for the conclusion that [□Triple-O] is possibly instantiated, the proponent of the conjunctive strategy has only gotten us to the conclusion that no non-God thing instantiates [□Triple-O]. But that tells us nothing at all positive about God. It is very far from entailing that God is omniscient, or omnipotent, or perfectly good; it only rules out the bizarre hypothesis that something other than God has these attributes.

At this stage, the defender of the conjunctive strategy might be tempted by the following reply to the preceding line of argument:

The argument of this section is an attempt to show that [Triple-O], and the conjunctive properties which follow on the march toward [□Triple-O], each can be trumped and hence fail to satisfy the second conjunct of [P2]. But this argument requires that the trumping properties be possibly instantiated; the second conjunct of [P2], after all, only requires that, for the candidate divine attribute in question, there is no *possible* being without the property which is greater than the one which has it. Our final trumping property was [□Triple-O]. But now you are objecting that we have been given no good reason to believe that [□Triple-O] is possible. Isn't this self-undermining?

Well, in a way, yes. But not in a way which is any help to the alethic perfect being theologian. For suppose that some of the alleged trumping properties produced in the course of our argument are not possibly instantiated. Which ones? Alethic perfect being theology gives us no help in answering this question. And because it gives us no help here, it gives us no help in figuring out which of these (if any) is among the divine attributes. Given [GPB], we know that, if it is any of these, it must be the best possibly instantiated one; but we have no idea which one this is.

But the proponent of the conjunctive strategy is not yet out of moves. Let's consider a few ways in which the proponent of that strategy might try to secure a more interesting result than the one just sketched.

### 2.4.1 The conjunctive-disjunctive strategy

One promising thought begins with the point that, while the proponent of the claim that God is the greatest possible being has not yet earned the right to the claim that God has the GIP-property described above—namely [□Triple-O]—she is at least entitled to the conclusion that God has at least one GIP-property. And, for all that has been said, perhaps all GIP-properties agree in attributing to God [Triple-O], or something quite like it.

With this in mind, the proponent of the conjunctive strategy might reason as follows: if God is the greatest possible being, then God has at least one GIP-property. So let's consider the disjunction of all of the GIP-properties. If God's possessing this disjunctive property entails that God is, for example, omnipotent, we are then entitled to conclude, via alethic perfect being reasoning, that God is omnipotent. Call this the conjunctive-disjunctive strategy.

The key question then is: is there any interesting property $F$ such that, for any GIP-property, we can see that anything with the GIP-property would also be $F$? If the answer to this question is 'Yes,' then the proponent of the conjunctive strategy has a reply to the argument of the preceding section.

The central problem for the conjunctive-disjunctive strategy comes from the diversity of GIP-properties. For consider the property described by the following story:

Demos is a necessarily existing being, and necessarily creates the universe. Demos is essentially good, but not perfectly good. And, while Demos is essentially quite powerful—much more powerful than any being with which we are acquainted—Demos is not omnipotent. There are strict limits to the sorts of universes Demos can create. Further, Demos knows much about the universe it creates—more, for example, than any human being knows—but not everything. But Demos knows enough never to create a universe which could give rise to being which knows more, or is better in any respect, than itself.

Let us say that any being which has the properties attributed to Demos by the above story is 'Demosian.' It seems plausible that being Demosian is a GIP-property. If it is possibly instantiated, it is necessarily instantiated; and, in any world in which something is Demosian, that thing is the greatest being in that world. If this is right, then the conjunctive-disjunctive strategy can't deliver the conclusions that God is omnipotent, or perfectly good, or omniscient, for being Demosian is a GIP-property, and Demosian beings are neither omnipotent nor perfectly good nor omniscient.

One may object that this sort of worry involves views which no one nowadays takes at all seriously. But this objection is not on very firm ground. Consider, for example, the deist hypothesis which exerted such a powerful influence on many of the most advanced scientific thinkers of the seventeenth and eighteenth centuries. If Deism were true, as many thought, and also necessarily true, then the greatest possible being would be a creator of the universe, but not clearly especially concerned with the goings on in that universe, once created. It would not be that far off of a Demosian being.

But perhaps, even if the conjunctive-disjunctive strategy can't give us everything, it can still deliver something. After all, it is not as though the intersection of the properties entailed by [□Triple-O] and those entailed by the property of being Demosian is empty. Both plausibly entail, for example, that the greatest possible being is the creator of the universe. Can the conjunctive-disjunctive strategy at least deliver the result that God is the creator of the universe?

I doubt it. Consider the following story:

The universe began, and necessarily began, in a formless chaos. This chaos necessarily gives rise to Olympian beings who, while quite powerful, are occasionally capricious, and do not in general know what the others are planning. The greatest of these is Zeus, who rules the others . . .

Let us say that any being that has all the properties attributed to Zeus in the above story—being necessarily formed out of chaos, ruling the other Olympian gods—is 'Zeusian.' It seems plausible that being Zeusian is a GIP-property. If it is possibly instantiated, it is necessarily instantiated; and, in any world in which something is Zeusian, that thing is the greatest being in that world. But if something is Zeusian, it did not create the universe; so the conjunctive-disjunctive strategy does not deliver the conclusion that God created the universe.

The recipe here is pretty clear: we begin with some cosmogony other than that provided by classical theism, and then add in appropriate modal assumptions to give us the necessity of relevant aspects of the creation story. This will then, so to speak, 'shrink modal space' so that the greatest possible being—the greatest being in that shrunken modal space—is a being quite unlike a being with [□Triple-O].[21]

Can the perfect being theologian at least infer that God is as great a Zeusian being? That at least seems to be entailed by possession of the disjunctive property

[□Triple-O] ∨ Demosian ∨ Zeusian

But it is fairly obvious that the story of Zeus can simply be modified to give Zeus less and less power—and as Zeus' powers shrink, so does modal space, and the greatness of the greatest possible being.

Of course, we can't make Zeus less great than the greatest actual being, since then our knowledge of the actual world would entail the impossibility of the relevant scenario. But that just means that the conjunctive-disjunctive strategy cannot deliver more than the meager results delivered by the combination of [G$\alpha$B] and [$\alpha$2], discussed in §2.1 above.

Nor, presumably, are stories like this the end of the line. They just provide a way to illustrate the massive range and diversity of GIP-properties. Other views of modal space provide different ways to show that GIP-properties might turn out to be rather unimpressive, even if they do not provide explicit examples of GIP-properties. Here is an example, which we might call 'Singularity':

---

[21] For more discussion of this phenomenon of the 'shrinking of modal space'—and of the sense in which this phenomenon is a feature of many monotheistic, and, in particular, Christian cosmogonies—see §6.3 below.

The universe, of necessity, begins with expansion from a high density singularity. Everything that exists is causally 'downstream' from this singularity. In different worlds, the universe unfolds differently—partly due to variation in the laws of nature, and partly due to chance. But the laws can only vary in a tight band, and it is impossible for the laws to be such as to permit the evolution of organisms significantly more intelligent or powerful than human beings.

One cannot read off a GIP-property from this description of the universe—but one can see that, if Singularity is true, no possible GIP-property will attribute its bearer anything much like the properties traditionally attributed to God.

In sum: the range of GIP-properties seems to rule out the conjunctive-disjunctive strategy, since the disjunction of the GIP-properties seems to entail nothing of interest about the greatest possible being.

### 2.4.2 The conjunctive-elimination strategy

Let's try a different tack. Rather than simply disjoining the GIP-properties and trying to see what follows from a being's satisfying the resulting disjunction, the proponent of the conjunctive strategy might try to eliminate some of the GIP-properties. Perhaps independent arguments show that superficially coherent properties like being Demosian or being Zeusian can, on closer examination, be seen to be impossible. If the alethic perfect being theologian can eliminate enough GIP-properties in this way, she might be left with a core collection of GIP-properties whose disjunction *does* entail an interesting claim about God. And there is nothing in perfect being theology which says that it can't be supplemented by additional 'impossibility' arguments of that sort. Call this the conjunctive-elimination strategy.

But this strategy faces a dilemma. Either the elimination of rogue GIP-properties will proceed 'one-by-one', or it will involve general arguments for the conclusion that no property which does not involve some interesting perfection could be a GIP-property.

The first approach—given the number and diversity of GIP-properties—seems hopeless. So suppose that we take the second route, and imagine that we put together an argument for the conclusion that no property which does not entail, for example, omnipotence, is a possibly instantiated GIP-property. That argument will have as its conclusion

Necessarily, if $x$ instantiates a GIP-property, then $x$ is omnipotent.

If we had a good independent argument for this conclusion, then this argument would—by itself—show that omnipotence is a property of the greatest possible being. We would then have no need of [P2] or any other greatness condition. So while an argument of this sort would solve our problem, it would also include the very thing we have been trying, and so far failing, to find: a way to show that a given property is a property of the greatest possible being. Hence it would be less a supplement to the present version of alethic perfect being theology than a replacement for it.

There is of course no reason why the perfect being theologian cannot try to find such a replacement. But we can hardly defend an alethic perfect being theology based on [P2] by pointing out that we could derive the divine attributes using it if only we had a separate and independent way to carry out that very derivation.

### 2.4.3 The conjunctive-conceivability strategy

Here's a last move for the proponent of the conjunctive strategy:

We can grant that there are a wide diversity of GIP-properties which have very little in common, and that there is no way of ruling out a suitable number of these without having an independent argument for the conclusion that we wanted our perfect being argument to establish. But note that, of all of the GIP-properties which one can call to mind, [□Triple-O] is clearly the *best*. A being with [□Triple-O] would be far greater, for example, than a Demosian or Zeusian being. So God must have [□Triple-O].

I agree with everything in this line of thought until the last sentence. For (to repeat a familiar thought) it simply doesn't follow from the claim that [□Triple-O] is the greatest of all GIP-properties that the greatest possible being would have [□Triple-O]; that requires also the (trivializing) assumption that [□Triple-O] is possibly instantiated.

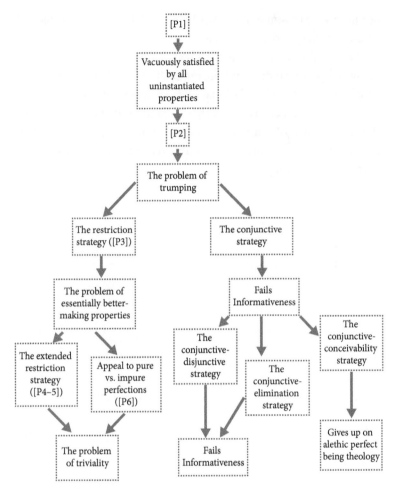

VARIETIES OF ALETHIC PERFECT BEING THEOLOGY AND THEIR DISCONTENTS

But this point does not undermine all views which someone who finds the above line of thought persuasive might have. For that person is likely tacitly ascribing to God a level of greatness greater than that accorded to God by [GPB]. She is likely, in particular, to have in mind the thesis that God is not just the greatest among all possible beings, but also the greatest among all conceivable beings. And even if we are not licensed to assume that God's being [□Triple-O] is possible, it is surely in some good sense conceivable.

The intuition that God is the greatest imaginable or conceivable being is a powerful one, and the argument from that premise to the conclusion that God has [□Triple-O] is a plausible one. But to endorse this line of argument is evidently to abandon alethic perfect being theology in favor of some version of epistemic perfect being theology. Let's now turn to the prospects for this second main version of pure perfect being theology.

# 3

# Epistemic Perfect Being Theology

The last chapter surveyed the significant difficulties which various versions of alethic perfect being theology face. I suspect that many readers will have been impatient with this catalogue, and will have wanted for some time to examine the prospects of an epistemic perfect being theology—one based on the claim that God is the greatest conceivable, rather than merely the greatest possible, being:

[GCB]   $[\forall x\colon x \neq \text{God}]\ \forall c \in C\ (\text{God}_\alpha > x_c)$

This is, after all, closer to the original Anselmian claim that God is a being than which no greater can be thought. And, as we'll see, epistemic perfect being theologies seem well-placed to solve at least some of the problems discussed above.

Recall that $c$, $c^*$ are variables over conceivable worlds, which may or may not be possible. When it is more convenient to express claims about conceivability using operators, I will use '$\blacklozenge$' and '$\blacksquare$' to express the analogues of '$\lozenge$' and '$\square$', so that '$\blacklozenge p$' is true iff $p$ is conceivable, and '$\blacksquare p$' is true iff $p$ is true in every conceivable world—if, that is, it is inconceivable that $p$ be false.

As with alethic perfect being theologies, the first step in providing an epistemic perfect being theology is to state a greatness condition: some condition on properties which is such that it follows from [GCB] that any property which satisfies this condition is a property of God.

## 3.1 Epistemic greatness conditions

A natural starting point is the condition a property satisfies iff, for any pair of conceivable beings, the one with the property is greater than the one without it:

[C1]   $\forall x \forall y \,((Fx_c \,\&\, \neg Fy_{c*}) \to x_c > y_{c*})$

But it is a familiar point from Chapter 2 that [C1], like [$\alpha$1] and [P1], fails the [Entailment] condition, because it is vacuously satisfied by any property which is not conceivably instantiated.

Better instead to model our greatness condition on one of the alethic greatness conditions which meet [Entailment]. The first of these was [P2], which differs from the above only in stipulating that the relevant property be possibly instantiated. Here, though, we can make do with the weaker assumption that the relevant property be conceivably instantiated:

[C2]   $\blacklozenge \exists x Fx \,\&\, \forall x \forall y \,((Fx_c \,\&\, \neg Fy_{c*}) \to x_c > y_{c*})$

A second option is based on [P5], which limits the entities to be compared to possible states of God:

[C3]   $\blacklozenge$(God is $F$) & (($F(\text{God})_c$ & $\neg F(\text{God})_{c*}$ & $<\text{God}_c, \text{God}_{c*}>$ are $F$-duplicates) $\to \text{God}_c > \text{God}_{c*}$)

By focusing on [C3]/[P5] for the moment, we can see some of the advantages of the move from an alethic to an epistemic perfect being theology.

Recall that the central problem with [P5] was that, given the truth of [□GPB], we never have a possible world in which God is $F$, and a possible world in which God is not $F$, and an asymmetry between the two worlds as regards God's greatness. There is thus no place for 'perfect being' reasoning to get a foothold. However, even if [□GPB] is true, it still might be that it is *conceivable* both that God is $F$ and that God is not $F$—even if God is greater if $F$ than if not $F$. And if God is not just the greatest possible, but also the greatest conceivable being, this fact could then help us to decide between the hypotheses that God is $F$ and that God is not $F$. Crucially, our stronger modal principle would avoid our having to make the trivializing assumption that it is possible that God is $F$ (or not $F$).

Now, this will be a non-starter if God is not just the greatest conceivable being, but also cannot be conceived to be anything less than the greatest conceivable being. For that would allow us to generate a principle which is the analogue of [□GPB]:

[■GCB]  $\forall x \forall c \forall c^* \neg (x_c > \text{God}_{c^*})$

Anselm, for one, seems inclined to endorse a principle of this sort.[1] If true, this principle would lead to just the same problems as the alethic perfect being theologian faced. For if [■GCB] is true, it follows that

$\forall c \forall c^* \neg (\text{God}_c > \text{God}_{c^*})$

But then, for any property $F$ such that God would be greater if $F$ than if not $F$, it will be inconceivable either that God is $F$ or that God is not $F$. And then the problems which arose for [P5] would have re-emerged in a new form.

But it seems to me that it is not implausible that this worry can be surmounted, because it is much more attractive to deny [■GCB] than to deny [□GPB]. For to deny [■GCB] is not to say that God *could* have been anything less than the greatest conceivable being; it is just to say that we can conceive of, or imagine, this being so. And the mere fact that we can conceive of this is, perhaps, not to deny any perfection of God.[2]

---

[1] He says (*Proslogion* §§II–III) that God cannot be conceived not to exist, and it would be a bit odd for him to hold this and to hold that God can be conceived to exist, but be less great than God actually is. Though again it bears stressing that Anselm is not, at least on the surface, employing any sort of distinction between conceivability and possibility.

[2] Although one can imagine a kind of 'perfect being' argument in favor of [■GCB]: wouldn't it be greater for God to be such that it is not even conceivable that God is less than the greatest conceivable being? And one can't block this by insisting that this property is impossible, if one genuinely thinks that God is the greatest conceivable being. One would have to hold that the property is not just impossible, but also (in whatever is the relevant sense) not conceivably instantiated.

The central question pressed in the last chapter was the question of what sort of greatness condition the alethic perfect being theologian should opt for. By contrast, here I won't focus on the question of whether [C2] or [C3] is the right way to go. (I'll use [C3] in what follows.) The key question for the epistemic perfect being theologian is: how should 'conceivable' be understood, as it is used in [GCB] and either of these greatness conditions?

## 3.2 The main problem

Below I will consider a number of ways in which the epistemic perfect being theologian might try to answer this question. But because the options are numerous, it is worth laying out in advance of a catalogue of proposed definitions the basic problem which I think faces any version of epistemic perfect being theology.

The problem can be presented as a dilemma. There are two constraints on the epistemic perfect being theologian's interpretation of 'conceivable,' and no interpretation of 'conceivable'—at least, none that I have been able to come up with—satisfies both.

The first constraint is perhaps obvious: if there is to be any difference between epistemic and alethic perfect being theologies, there must be some space between conceivability and possibility; it must be the case that $\blacklozenge p$ is sometimes true even when $\lozenge p$ is not. If this were not the case, then epistemic perfect being theology would collapse into alethic perfect being theology.

The second constraint is less obvious, but equally non-negotiable. Let us say that a property $F$ is a *trouble-maker* if it satisfies the following three conditions:

(i)  God would be better if $F$ than if not $F$.
(ii)  It is conceivable that God is $F$.
(iii)  It is not possible that God is $F$.

It is best not to think of (i)–(iii) as defining a class of properties. Instead, think of these conditions as a schema for defining a class of properties, instances of which are obtained by supplying a definition for 'conceivable.' So claims which follow to the effect that this or that property is a trouble-maker should be understood as claims about what properties are trouble-makers for certain definitions of 'conceivable.'

Now suppose for reductio that our epistemic perfect being theologian defines 'conceivable' in such a way that there is at least one trouble-maker. Then it follows from condition (i), [GCB], and our greatness condition that if it is conceivable that God is $F$, then God is $F$. From this and the fact that $F$ satisfies (ii) it follows that God is $F$. But it follows from (iii) that it is impossible that God is $F$, which is a contradiction.

What this shows is that, for any definition of 'conceivable' on which there are trouble-makers, the principle that God is the greatest conceivable being (on that interpretation of 'conceivable') will be false.

The task for the epistemic perfect being theologian, then, is to find a definition of 'conceivable' on which there is genuine space between conceivability and possibility, but not so much space as to let in trouble-makers. Let's look now at a few attempts to do just that.

## 3.3 Varieties of conceivability

A first step towards identifying the epistemic perfect being theologian's most promising options begins with a now-standard distinction between positive and negative conceivability.[3] To say that $p$ is positively conceivable is to say that one can, in some sense or other, imagine $p$ to be the case; it is to say that one has the positive ability to be in a certain kind of mental state with $p$ as its content. To say that a claim is negatively conceivable, by contrast, is to say that $p$ is (in a sense to be specified) unable to be ruled out. A claim can be negatively conceivable even if we can form no positive conception at all of what the world would have to be like for that claim to be true.

[3] The distinction in this form is due to Chalmers (2002); it is related to one drawn in van Cleve (1983).

I suggest that by far the more promising route for the epistemic perfect being theologian is to frame her characteristic theses in terms of some sort of negative conceivability. The reason is just that it is not easy to see what it would mean to positively conceive of the sorts of theses in which we are interested. What would it mean, for instance, to positively conceive of God's being omnipotent, or perfectly good? Certainly we can't imagine these claims being true in any straightforward sense. By contrast, it is easy to see how claims like this might be negatively conceivable, if a certain kind of reasoning is unable to rule them out.

Supposing that this is correct, and that the epistemic perfect being theologian should understand [GCB] and the relevant greatness condition in terms of negative conceivability, I think that we can usefully divide varieties of negative conceivability which the epistemic perfect being theologian might exploit into two. The first explicates this notion in terms of some sort of logical consistency; on this view, a claim is conceivable if, in some sense, it cannot be logically ruled out. The second explicates this notion in terms of some broader epistemic notion; on one promising approach of this sort, a claim is conceivable iff it cannot be ruled out on a priori grounds. Let's look at a few different instances of each strategy.

### 3.3.1 Conceivability and logical truth

The simplest way to define conceivability in terms of logical truth would be the following:

$p$ is conceivable$_1$ iff $\neg p$ is not a formal logical truth.[4]

---

[4] Here and in what follows I'm being a bit sloppy about the distinction between propositions and sentences. For presumably the things that are conceivable or not are propositions, whereas the things that are formal logical truths are sentences. The defender of the view being sketched in the text, if in possession of a sufficiently fine-grained view of propositions, might resolve the difficulty by saying that, in an extended sense, a proposition is a formal logical truth if it is expressed by at least one sentence which is a formal logical truth. I don't think that for present purposes much hangs on the details here.

On this interpretation, the claim that a certain hypothesis about God is conceivable will be an extremely weak claim. On the one hand, this is a good thing, for it gives us the space for perfect being reasoning to do some work; it is not difficult to find contrary theses about God which are both plainly conceivable$_1$.

But this virtue corresponds to a vice. Interpreting 'conceivable' as expressing conceivability$_1$ makes the claim that God is the greatest conceivable being—the core of any epistemic perfect being theology—implausibly strong. This is because it entails the existence of trouble-makers. To see this, consider Descartes' question of whether God 'was free to make it not true that all the radii of the circle are equal.'[5] Descartes is asking whether God has a property like

CIRCLE.   $x$ can make the radii of a circle unequal

Our question is: is CIRCLE a trouble-maker?

Let's look at the three conditions on trouble-makers. The easiest of these is condition (ii), which asks whether it is conceivable$_1$ that God have CIRCLE. The answer to this question is clearly 'Yes,' since the negation of that claim that God can make the radii of a circle unequal is not a formal logical truth.

While I will return to this below, I think that it is also very plausible that CIRCLE satisfies condition (iii): it is not possible that God have this property. The reason is familiar: if it were possible, then it would be possible for God to make the radii of a circle unequal; but if this were possible, then it would be possible for there to be a circle with unequal radii; but this is impossible.

Let's turn then to the key question, which is whether CIRCLE satisfies condition (i). This is the question whether, all things being equal, it would be greater for God to have this property than to lack it. I think that a strong case can be made that the answer to this question is 'Yes.'

Anyone who has ever taught philosophy of religion to undergraduates knows how powerful the intuitions are which underwrite the

---

[5] Letter to Mersenne, 27 May 1630.

Cartesian conception of omnipotence. In my experience, almost to a person, students initially find repugnant the idea that God could be, as they put it, 'limited by the laws of logic' or 'limited by mathematical facts.'

Of course, students can be talked out of this. But they are not talked out of this by being convinced that a power like CIRCLE would not be better to have than lack. Rather, they are talked out of it by reasoning of the following sort:

Yes, it would be an awesome thing to be able to make the radii of a circle unequal. But in the end, the idea that a thing could have a property like CIRCLE is incoherent. For if a thing could have this property, then it would be possible for that thing to make a circle with radii of unequal lengths; and then it would be possible for a circle to have radii of unequal lengths. And this is obviously incoherent. But we shouldn't attribute properties to God which lead to incoherence in this way, and it is no mark against the greatness of God for God to lack properties which turn out, in the end, to be impossible for anything to have.

That is, they are convinced, not that CIRCLE would not be a great property to have, but that it is impossible for even God to have it, and that there is nothing wrong with denying even quite impressive-seeming properties to God if it is impossible for anything to have those properties.

But speeches like the one just imagined don't sit well in the mouth of the epistemic perfect being theologian. After all, nothing in this speech blocks our argument that CIRCLE is a trouble-maker for conceivability$_1$. The speech concedes that it would be greater to have CIRCLE than to lack it, and hence concedes that CIRCLE satisfies condition (i) in our definition of a trouble-maker. It is simply argued that, despite this, because the supposition that God has CIRCLE leads to incoherence, we can reasonably deny that God has this property.

There is, in my view, nothing wrong with this piece of reasoning. But it is not a defense of the present version of epistemic perfect being theology; instead, it is simply a way of denying that God is the greatest conceivable$_1$ being.

A similar point could be made about the following attempt to block the result that CIRCLE is a trouble-maker:

We have already seen that it is incoherent to suppose that anything instantiates CIRCLE. But if it is incoherent to suppose that anything has this property, then it *can't* be better to have this property than to lack it. It is never better to have an impossible property than to lack it.

But this is (again) a barely concealed return to alethic perfect being theology. If we are to stipulate from the start that only possibly instantiated properties can be better to have than lack, then we are restricting our comparisons of relative greatness to beings in genuinely possible worlds. And that makes [C2] and [C3] notational variants of, respectively, [P2] and [P5].

Let's turn to a different way in which the proponent of the 'conceivable$_1$' interpretation might resist the argument that CIRCLE is a trouble-maker. This would be to simply agree with Descartes that God does have this property, and hence deny that CIRCLE satisfies condition (iii) in the definition of a trouble-maker. Perhaps the most plausible way to do this is to deny that ability entails possibility, and so deny that God's instantiating CIRCLE entails that it is possible for the radii of a circle to be unequal—thus blocking the argument that God's having this property would be incoherent.[6]

As many have noted, it is hard to deny that ability does entail possibility, just because it is hard to see how someone could be able to do something if it is literally impossible for them, no matter what, to do it. But in the present context a more direct reply is available, since it is also plainly conceivable$_1$ that God have the property

$x$ possibly makes the radii of a circle unequal

and this, like CIRCLE, seems like a property which is, all else equal, better to have than to lack. Hence it seems, whatever we say about the relation between ability and possibility, to be a trouble-maker.[7]

---

[6] This interpretation of Descartes is defended in Kaufman (2002) and Newlands (2013).

[7] Another move would be to simply bite the bullet, and accept the conclusion that it is possible for the radii of a circle to be unequal. (This is, on the reading of Frankfurt

Let's take a step back. I have been arguing that, if 'conceivability' means 'conceivability$_1$,' then CIRCLE is a trouble-maker. And this implies that, if our modal principle—that God is the greatest conceivable$_1$ being—is true, then God instantiates CIRCLE. But God does not instantiate CIRCLE. So, the claim that God is the greatest conceivable$_1$ being is false.

Many proponents of epistemic perfect being theology will by this point be anxious to move on from conceivability$_1$. I have somewhat belabored the problems with this definition of conceivability in order to make vivid the dilemma presented in §3.2 above. We began with a definition of conceivability which makes room for claims which are conceivable but not possible; but this definition also appears to make room for trouble-makers. We considered various ways of arguing that, contrary to appearance, properties like CIRCLE are not trouble-makers; but these lines of response turn on the denial that impossible properties can ever be better to have than lack, which collapses epistemic into alethic perfect being theology. This oscillation between the two horns of our dilemma will, as we'll see, recur when we turn to other, superficially more promising, accounts of conceivability.

As suggested above, the right thing for the epistemic perfect being theologian to say is that conceivability$_1$ is simply too weak a notion to do the required work. The class of formal logical truths seems, in the present context, far too sparse to appropriately limit the hypotheses about God which we wish to consider as live options. Suppose for now that we want to stick with a definition of conceivability which defines it in terms of some sort of formal truth. A reasonable thought would be to strengthen our definition in such a way as to make it inconceivable that mathematical facts—like the fact that all the radii of the circle are equal—be other than they are. So we might try

(1977), Descartes' view.) On this view CIRCLE would not satisfy condition (iii) in the definition of trouble-makers. It is hard to know what to say about this move, other than to point out that it is also conceivable$_1$ that God have properties like the one corresponding to the open sentence

$x$ can make $1 \neq 1$

and that it is just very hard to believe that it is possible that $1 \neq 1$.

$p$ is conceivable$_2$ iff $\neg p$ is not a logical consequence of a logical or mathematical truth.

This might appear promising, since one might make a case that the claim

God can make the radii of the circle unequal

is not conceivable$_2$, on the grounds that it entails that it is possible that the radii of the circle be unequal, and the negation of this claim is a mathematical truth. If this were correct, then CIRCLE would not be a trouble-maker. And yet conceivability$_2$ is still a weak enough notion to allow plenty of space between conceivability and possibility. It is, to return to the example discussed in §2.3, conceivable$_2$ both that God does and that God does not explain the modal truths. Could conceivability$_2$ be the middle ground between conceivability$_1$ and possibility that we want?

Unfortunately not. For one thing, it does not even quite handle the case of CIRCLE. The negation of the claim that it is *possible* that the radii of the circle be unequal is not a mathematical truth; it is the negation of a modal claim about a mathematical truth. And, even setting this point to the side, conceivability$_2$ is powerless to handle variants of the radii/circle case, like—to use another of Descartes' examples[8]—

God can make a mountain without a valley

This is clearly conceivable$_2$. And, as above, it seems plausible that, all else equal, it is greater for God to have this ability than to lack it. So, the property

$x$ can make a mountain without a valley

is a trouble-maker for conceivability$_2$, and hence is a property of the greatest conceivable$_2$ being. And this is just a reductio of the claim that God is the greatest conceivable$_2$ being.

We're exploring the possibility of defining conceivability in terms of consistency with a certain class of truths. The failure of our previous

---

[8] Letter to Arnauld, 29 July 1648.

two attempts show that the class of formal logical and mathematical truths is too narrow. The example of a mountain without a valley makes it tempting to define conceivability in terms of consistency with the necessary truths, as follows:

$p$ is conceivable$_3$ iff $\neg p$ is not a logical consequence of a necessary truth.

But this would just reinstate the problems of alethic perfect being theology, since—given that every necessary truth is a logical consequence of itself—conceivability$_3$ is trivially coextensive with possibility.

What is needed is some restricted class of necessary truths, so that some truths which turn out to be impossible might nonetheless not be logical consequences of truths in the restricted class. Adopting an idea from Brian Leftow, we might focus on the class of secular necessary truths—intuitively, truths that don't say anything about God.[9] This would give us:

$p$ is conceivable$_4$ iff $\neg p$ is not a logical consequence of a secular necessary truth.

But this neglects a problem which was already present in our earlier formulations, which is that the logical consequence relation is too weak to do the intended work. Think about how the present proposal is meant to handle the case of a mountain without a valley. The idea is that it is a secular necessary truth that there cannot be a mountain without a valley; and it is a consequence of this necessary truth that God cannot make a mountain without a valley. For this reason, the argument goes, the claim that God can make a mountain without a valley is not conceivable.

The problem is that the consequence relation which figures in this piece of reasoning is not a logical one. It is not a logical consequence of the claim that there cannot be a mountain without a valley that God cannot make a mountain without a valley. Indeed, it is not even an analytic entailment, as presumably the principle that ability entails

---

[9] See Leftow (2012, 2015). Leftow gives a more precise characterization of the secular truths; more on this below.

possibility is, even if necessary, synthetic. The worry, then, is that God's being able to make a mountain without a valley might, for all we have said, still be conceivable$_4$.

To block this, one might say that the fact that ability entails possibility is itself a secular necessary truth. Given that the conjunction of a pair of secular necessary truths is presumably itself a secular necessary truth, the following would also appear to be a secular necessary truth:

It is impossible that there be a mountain without a valley and $\forall x \forall p$
(If $x$ is able to bring about $p$, then $p$ is possible)

Presuming (as we have been) that we can make sense of relations of logical consequence between propositions, it is at least reasonably plausible that it is a logical consequence of this conjunction that God cannot create a mountain without a valley. And this implies that it is not conceivable$_4$ that God create a mountain without a valley, which is just the result we sought.

But this move, while initially promising, simply underscores the difficulty in giving an account of what the secular truths are. Our conjunctive proposition includes a universal quantifier, and the domain of this quantifier must (to secure the wanted logical consequence) include God. Should propositions which quantify over such domains count as secular, or not? Either way there is trouble.

If they are not secular, then the above conjunction is not a secular necessary truth, and we are left without a reply to the problem that the property of making a mountain without a valley is a trouble-maker for conceivability$_4$.

So suppose instead they are secular. Then (again) conceivability$_4$ collapses into possibility, and we fall back into the problem that we cannot tell whether claims of interest are conceivable without first knowing whether they are true. Recall the familiar point that if God is better if $F$ than if not $F$, then either the claim that God is $F$ or its negation will be a necessary truth. But now consider the quantified claims that something is $F$ and its negation. These will both by the present standard be secular. But for most properties of interests— which will be properties of God or of nothing—they will also be necessary if true. But that means that, in cases of interest, either the claim that God is $F$ or its negation will be inconsistent with a secular necessary truth, and hence inconceivable$_4$. We can know which is conceivable$_4$ only by knowing which is possible; and, for reasons already belabored, the relevant possibility claims are trivially equivalent to the theses for which we were trying to argue.

We are trying to define a workable notion of conceivability in terms of consistency with some class of truths. Perhaps the moral of the chain of argument to this point is that we need to frame that definition in terms of some relation stronger than strictly logical consistency. The restriction to logical consequence, after all, is what forces us to appeal to the universally quantified proposition which proved problematic for conceivability$_4$.

A natural suggestion, which would yield the wanted result that it is not conceivable that God can make a mountain without a valley, is to move from logical consequence to simple entailment:

$p$ is conceivable$_5$ iff $\neg p$ is not entailed by a secular necessary truth.

But a moment's inspection shows that conceivability$_5$, like conceivability$_3$, simply collapses conceivability into possibility, and so epistemic into alethic perfect being theology. Every necessary truth is entailed by everything, and so in particular is entailed by some secular necessary truth.

Could we instead appeal to some restricted entailment relation, which is weaker than logical consequence but stronger than simple entailment? Suppose that we define some such notion; call it $R$-entailment. That would give us

$p$ is conceivable$_6$ iff $\neg p$ is not $R$-entailed by a secular necessary truth.

I think that, even in advance of being given details about $R$-entailment, we can see that this attempt is unlikely to succeed. The central problem comes from claims like this one:

God can make something which is red and uncolored.

This had better come out as inconceivable$_6$. Were this not the case, then, since (I presume) this is not a possible property of God, and yet is (for reasons parallel to those discussed above) better to have than lack, the property of being able to make something which is red and uncolored would be a trouble-maker for conceivability$_6$.

So is it inconceivable$_6$? The best argument that it is begins with the point that, even in advance of details, we know that $R$-entailment must be a weak enough relation that ability claims $R$-entail the corresponding possibility claims. (Otherwise, it would be powerless to handle the kinds of cases already discussed.) Further, we are assuming that the following is true:

It is impossible for there to be something red and uncolored.

And this $R$-entails the negation of the claim that God can make something red and uncolored. So why is this not enough to give us the wanted result that this claim is inconceivable$_6$?

The central problem is one which we already discussed in connection with conceivability$_4$. Either universally quantified claims are secular or they are not. If they are, then (for reasons discussed above) a definition of conceivability in terms of secular truth will collapse conceivability into possibility. If they are not, then the claim that there is not something which is red and uncolored is, while necessary, not secular. Hence the fact that its necessity $R$-entails that God cannot make something which is red and uncolored does not suffice to render the claim that God can make something red and uncolored inconceivable$_6$. And, as far as I can see, there are not any other necessary truths which are better candidates to be secular which could play this role.

It is reasonable, at this point, to be pessimistic about the chances of finding a notion of conceivability definable in terms of consistency with some class of truths which is suitable for the purposes of the epistemic perfect being theologian. It is time to try another approach.

### 3.3.2 Conceivability and a priori truth

The problems encountered so far all point in the same direction: we need a yet more restrictive sense of conceivability, such that claims like the claim that God could have made a mountain without a valley don't come out as, in the relevant sense, conceivable. The natural way to secure that result is to move from an account of conceivability in terms of consistency with some class of truths to an account of conceivability given in broader epistemic terms.

A familiar starting point would define conceivability in terms of the a priori, as follows:

$p$ is conceivable$_7$ iff $\neg p$ is not knowable a priori.

If it is a priori knowable that the radii of a circle must be equal, and knowable a priori that there can be no mountain without a valley (and knowable a priori that ability entails possibility), then something like this appears to avoid all of the trouble-makers which plagued our definitions of conceivability in terms of logical or mathematical truth. But if, as is widely held, some claims are necessary but not a priori knowable, this will yet leave room for the possibility of conceivable$_7$ but not possible propositions—which is what we want.

But a moment's reflection shows that this definition permits the existence of trouble-makers quite similar to those discussed in the previous section; we can simply modify the Cartesian examples above to make trouble for the version of epistemic perfect being theology which employs conceivability$_7$. For suppose that 'Hesperus is Phosphorus' and 'Water is $H_2O$' are examples of the necessary a posteriori, and consider the claims

God can make Hesperus distinct from Phosphorus.
God can make something water without making it $H_2O$.

We presumably want these claims to be inconceivable$_7$, for just the same reason sketched above: all things being equal, each of these claims would make God greater than its negation. We don't want this fact to lead us to conclude that God can bring about impossibilities. But each of these claims is pretty clearly conceivable$_7$; after all, if it is not knowable a priori that Hesperus is Phosphorus, then it is not knowable a priori that it is impossible for Hesperus to be distinct from Phosphorus, and so not knowable a priori that God lacks the ability to make Hesperus distinct from Phosphorus—which is enough to make the above claims conceivable$_7$. Given the present definition of conceivability, then, the property of making Hesperus distinct from Phosphorus is a trouble-maker. And this is a reductio of the claim that God is the greatest conceivable$_7$ being.

Some recent work on metaphysical modality and the a priori, however, suggests a patch.[10] According to some two-dimensionalist treatments of modality, instances of the necessary a posteriori are due to the presence of certain sorts of expressions whose extension depends on facts about the world in a certain distinctive way. The details can be laid out in various ways; here I follow David Chalmers, who introduces the notion of a 'semantically neutral' expression as follows:

> An expression is semantically neutral roughly when its extension in any given possible world is independent of which scenario is actual.[11]

One can, and Chalmers does, give a more thorough characterization of this notion. But thinking about a few examples will suffice for our purposes.

Consider the name 'Hesperus.' This actually has the planet Venus in its extension. But we can imagine a scenario qualitatively like our own in which the brightest star in the evening sky was not Venus, and instead was some other celestial body. Suppose now that you learn that that scenario is in fact actual. It is plausible that you would, given that information, identify the other celestial body, and not Venus, as the reference of 'Hesperus.' In this sense, the extension of ordinary names depends on 'which scenario is actual,' which means that ordinary names are not semantically neutral. Parallel considerations show that natural kind terms like 'water' are not semantically neutral.

But consider, to use one of Chalmers' examples, the term 'zero.' It is not so clear that we can imagine a scenario qualitatively like our own which, considered as actual, would have the effect that we would take something other than the number zero to be the referent of 'zero.' So perhaps 'zero' is semantically neutral.

---

[10] Thanks to Brian Cutter for suggesting the possibility of this move.
[11] Chalmers (2012), 370.

This is just a sketch of a complicated picture; but it will be enough for present purposes.[12] According to the sort of view developed by Chalmers and others, cases in which a sentence's modal and epistemic profiles come apart—as in cases of the necessary a posteriori—are due to the presence of expressions which are not semantically neutral. And one can see why this thesis seems plausible: if, intuitively, one does not know which scenario is actual, one cannot know a priori what the extension of a term like 'Hesperus' is. And that might seem to explain why one cannot know a priori that Hesperus is Phosphorus, despite the fact that this is a necessary truth. The idea is then that if we restrict ourselves to sentences which contain only semantically neutral terms, modal and epistemic profiles always coincide, so that a claim is necessary iff it is a priori.

Suppose that this is all correct.[13] Then one might use this apparatus to solve the problem just posed for conceivability$_7$, by giving the following definition of conceivability:

$p$ is conceivable$_8$ iff (i) $\neg p$ is not knowable a priori and (ii) $p$ is expressible by a sentence which contains only semantically neutral terms.

This blocks the argument that being able to make Hesperus distinct from Phosphorus is a trouble-maker. The claim that God can make Hesperus distinct from Phosphorus is not expressible by a sentence which contains only semantically neutral terms; so this claim is not conceivable$_8$.

But, in a by-now familiar pattern, we have landed back on the other horn of our dilemma. For suppose, as we have been, that claims expressed by sentences containing only semantically neutral terms are necessary iff they are a priori. It follows immediately that any proposition which satisfies the definition of conceivability$_8$ is possible.

---

[12] For the most thorough working-out of this picture, see Chalmers (2012).

[13] My own view is that the best version of this sort of view ends up misclassifying certain a posteriori claims as a priori. I argue for this in Speaks (2010). But many would disagree. Here I just assume the adequacy of the framework for the sake of argument, to see whether it might be of use to the epistemic perfect being theologian.

But that (again) turns our attempt to construct a viable epistemic perfect being theology into a notational variant on alethic perfect being theology.

Suppose, to return to our example, that we want to know whether God explains the necessary truths. Either the sentence 'God explains the necessary truths' contains only semantically neutral terms or it does not. If it does not, then both this claim and its negation are inconceivable$_8$, and perfect being reasoning can't get off the ground. If it is semantically neutral, then, given that conceivability$_8$ entails possibility, and both the claim that God explains the necessary truths and its negation are necessary if true, exactly one of the claim that God explains the necessary truths and its negation is conceivable$_8$. So we will not have a pair of conceivable$_8$ hypotheses which [GCB] might help us to decide between. And, what's worse, the line of argument just sketched shows that for theses like these, conceivability$_8$ immediately entails truth, which is just the trivializing result we were trying to avoid.

This may seem like an odd result, since one might think that, intuitively, both the claim that God does and that God does not explain the necessary truths might be unable to be ruled out a priori. But if this were true, then these hypotheses about God would be counterexamples to the claim that necessity and a prioricity are coextensive when it comes to semantically neutral claims.[14] But if they were genuine counterexamples, we could use them to show that conceivability$_8$ generates trouble-makers.

For let G be some hypothesis about God such that it and its negation are conceivable$_8$ but which is such that G is true and its negation is impossible, and consider the proposition that God can bring about ¬G. This would seem to be conceivable$_8$, but impossible. And given that, intuitively, it will be greater for God to be able to bring

---

[14] Chalmers is aware that certain theses about a necessary God would provide apparent counterexamples to these equivalences; see, among other places, Chalmers (2012), 177–8.

about $\neg G$ than otherwise, this makes the proposition that God can bring about $\neg G$ a trouble-maker.

So either hypotheses about God are counterexamples to the general rule that semantically neutral claims are necessary iff a priori or they are not. If they are, we get trouble-makers. If they are not, we get the usual collapse into alethic perfect being theology.

What we want, it seems, is some definition of the following form

$p$ is conceivable$_9$ iff (i) $\neg p$ is not knowable a priori and (ii) . . .

where the ellipsis is filled in by some condition weaker than possibility. Might there be some way for the epistemic perfect being theologian to make this work, even if we can't think of it right now?

Here is an argument that there is not. Suppose for reductio that we have found a successful way of filling in our definition of conceivability$_9$. For it to be successful, we need to be able to use the principle that God is the greatest conceivable$_9$ being to decide between a pair of hypotheses $p, q$ which are both conceivable$_9$, but at least one of which is not possible. (If both were possible, we could stick with an alethic perfect being theology, and the principle that God is the greatest possible being—we would have no need to define the relevant sense of conceivability.) If $p, q$ are both conceivable$_9$, then neither is knowable a priori. So we have to be able to use the principle that God is the greatest conceivable$_9$ being to decide between a pair of hypotheses, neither of which is a priori. But presumably the principle that God is the greatest conceivable$_9$ being is knowable a priori, if knowable at all. And the argument from this principle to one of $p, q$ will be an a priori argument. And from this it follows that, contrary to our initial supposition, one of $p, q$ must be a priori, and hence that it is not the case that both are (whatever the details of our definition turn out to be) conceivable$_9$.

This appears to show that there is something self-undermining about the attempt to construct a definition of conceivability which is useful for the epistemic perfect being theologian out of the notion of a priori knowability. The problem is that a successful epistemic perfect being theology would deliver a priori knowledge of claims about God which must be assumed not to be knowable a priori for the method to get off the ground in the first place.[15]

Indeed, the point is more general than that. Pick any positive epistemic status $E$ which is such that perfect being theology is intended to confer $E$ on claims about the divine attributes. The form of argument just given shows that we cannot construct a workable definition of conceivability around the class of claims which lack $E$. This makes it hard to see how we could define the relevant sort of negative conceivability in broadly epistemic terms.

*    *    *

I have, obviously, not considered every conceivable definition of conceivability, and one might hope that another would fare better than those that I have considered. But, given the pattern exhibited by analyses of conceivability just considered, this seems to me quite unlikely. This is because the notion of conceivability, in the hands of the epistemic perfect being theologian, is subject to theoretical pressures which push in opposite directions.

On the one hand, if the move from an alethic to an epistemic perfect being theology is to do any work, then we need a notion of conceivability on which some impossibilities are conceivable. But, once we do this, it is hard, as the above examples show, to avoid the conclusion that there are some impossibilities which are in the relevant sense conceivable but which would make God greater than not. It is, that is, hard to avoid letting in trouble-makers.

And this pushes us in exactly the opposite direction, since to get rid of the trouble-makers one has to close off at least some of the space between conceivability and possibility. The aim of this chapter has been to show that there is no obvious way to do that without

---

[15] One might try to stipulate one's way around this problem by modifying the first condition to say something like '$\neg p$ is not knowable a priori except via reasoning from [GCB].' But this would be objectionably circular, since [GCB] contains the term for which we are trying to provide the definition. One might try instead something like 'except via reasoning from non-secular truths.' But this would reinstate the kinds of problems about delimiting the class of secular claims discussed in §3.3.1.

simply erasing that space altogether. And, if that is right, epistemic perfect being theology is no real alternative to alethic perfect being theology. The claim that God is the greatest conceivable being is either equivalent to the claim that God is the greatest possible being, or simply false.[16]

[16] It would be a mistake to read this as a serious criticism of Anselm and other writers in the tradition who claim that God is the greatest conceivable being, or greater than any being that can be imagined, for reasons discussed in Chapter 1, note 4: before Descartes, the distinction between conceivability and possibility seems to be rarely, if ever, explicitly made, which makes the attribution of an epistemic as opposed to alethic perfect being theology to thinkers like Anselm a bit tenuous.

# 4

# Impure Perfect Being Theology

In the last two chapters we have tried, and failed, to find a successful instance of pure perfect being theology. This would include a true modal principle, and a greatness condition which satisfied our twin constraints of [Entailment] and [Informativeness]. But even if you agree with the negative conclusion of those chapters, that does not mean that the constructive program of perfect being theology is dead in the water.

While many contemporary advocates of perfect being theology present their program in such a way as to suggest that they are deriving results about divine attributes from the claim that God is the greatest possible being, many in practice proceed in a more indirect way. Many don't argue directly for the claim that the greatest possible being would have this or that property. Instead, they assert that the greatest possible being would have every property meeting a certain description, and then argue that certain candidate attributes do meet that description.

Let's call this method *impure perfect being theology*. Instances of impure perfect being theology in effect conjoin the principle that God is the greatest possible being with some *bridge principle* of the form

If $x$ is the greatest possible being, then $x$ has every $G$-property

or

If $x$ is the greatest conceivable being, then $x$ has every $G$-property where the relevant instance of impure perfect being theology is defined by the choice of the class of G-properties. Often, the phrase 'great-making property' is used to single out the G-properties; but, since this phrase has a few different established meanings, I'll use the neutral 'G-properties' to single out the class of properties playing the relevant role in a theorist's chosen bridge principle.

There is a very clear sense in which advocates of impure perfect being theology are beginning with a more substantial conception of God than the modal conception of God. For each assumes from the outset, not just that God is the greatest actual, possible, or conceivable being, but also that God has all of the G-properties. This is so because each includes a bridge principle, and this bridge principle has the status of an independent assumption, not derivable from the claim that God is the greatest possible being. That already follows from the arguments of Chapters 2 and 3—for, if there were a way to derive a substantial bridge principle from one of our modal principles, then there would be a successful version of either alethic or epistemic perfect being theology. But, as we have seen, there isn't.

One might wonder, then, in what sense an impure perfect being theology counts as an instance of perfect being theology, thought of as the attempt to argue for theses about the divine attributes from the modal conception of God. What work in an impure perfect being theology is really being done by the principle that God is the greatest possible being? Why not just begin with the assumption that God has every G-property, and leave the modal conception of God behind?

This, however, would be too quick. Even if there is no straightforward argument from one of our modal principles to the conclusion that God has every G-property, the claim that God is the greatest possible being may still play the role of a kind of background assumption which makes the claim that God has every G-property seem plausible. Given this, it seems reasonable to expect a satisfactory definition of the G-properties to meet the following three desiderata:

[Plausibility]   It should be plausible that if *x* is the greatest possible being, then *x* has all of the G-properties. (That is, the relevant bridge principle should be plausible.)

[Informativeness]   We should be able to identify at least some interesting G-properties without relying on prior substantial assumptions about God.

[Adequacy]   It should not be the case that there are any G-properties which are not plausible candidates to be among the divine attributes.

If a definition of the G-properties did not meet [Plausibility], then there would be no reason—at least, no perfect being reason—to accept the claim that God has all of the G-properties. If it did not meet [Informativeness], then the relevant bridge principle would not tell us anything about God, and hence would not do the job for which it was introduced. If it did not meet [Adequacy], then we would know that not all G-properties are divine attributes—which would mean that, given [GPB], the relevant bridge principle is false.

The space of possible instances of impure perfect being theology is not limited in any obvious way; there are any number of possible bridge principles which one might offer. I won't pretend to discuss every possible definition which one might find plausible. But there are, I think, two main ways to go about defining the G-properties.

The distinction between them can be brought out by distinguishing between two different ways in which the greatness of a pair of beings might be compared. First, we might ask which of the beings is greater, full stop. This is the sort of relation between entities which, in the preceding chapters, was represented by '$<$.' The impure perfect being theologian might, first, try to formulate a bridge principle in terms of this relation. I'll call this the *absolute greatness* approach.

But this is not the only place one might begin. Just as we can compare the absolute greatness of a pair of beings, we might compare their greatness as members of a certain kind. These kinds of comparison are not the same. Some properties are good for me relative to a kind of which I am a member. For instance, I'm a member of the kind basketball player, and, relative to that kind, it is better for me to shoot baskets every day than not to—that is, I would be a better basketball player were I to shoot baskets every day, than were I not to. But this fact, even given that I am a member of that kind, doesn't entail that this property is one which it is better for me to have than lack, full stop. In fact, I don't think that it is. I'll call this sort of property *kind-relative greatness*.

This sort of property has not shown up so far; our pure versions of perfect being theology all employed kind-independent comparisons of absolute greatness. It is true that we did consider the strategy of restricting our quantification over relevant individuals to those of a certain kind (for example, persons). But to compare individuals of a certain kind for absolute greatness is not the same thing as asking which individuals are greater-for-that-kind than others. One basketball player may be greater (full stop) than another, even if the latter is a greater basketball player than the former. That is, in the notation above, it might be that

$x$ is a basketball player & $y$ is a basketball player & $x > y$

even if

$y$ is a greater basketball player than $x$

Given that we have so far neglected kind-relative greatness, it might appear to be an appealing strategy for the impure perfect being theologian to construct a bridge principle using this notion. She might, for instance, select some suitable kind $K$ and argue that God has all of the properties that would make something a better $K$. I'll call this the *kind-relative* approach.

## 4.1 Absolute greatness

The first sort of strategy can be thought of as starting with the basic notion of a property that it is better to have than lack. We might define this notion as follows:

$F$ is a better-making property for $x$ in $w$ iff (i) $x$ is $F$ in $w$ and (ii) the world $w^*$ most similar to $w$ in which $x$ lacks $F$ is such that $x_w > x_{w^*}$

So defined, being a better-making property is a three-place relation between a property, an individual, and a world. Let's ask whether we can use this sort of relation to define the $G$-properties.

The simplest versions of the attempt to define the $G$-properties in terms of the better-making properties are obvious, if instructive, failures. It will obviously fail [Adequacy] to say that

[G1]    $F$ is a $G$-property if it is better-making for something

Having excellent eyesight is a better-making feature for a hawk, and producing many seeds is a better-making property for an orange; but God neither has excellent eyesight nor produces many seeds.

Nor will it work to say that

[G2]    $F$ is a $G$-property if it is better-making for everything

since this will just land us back in problems familiar from our discussion of versions of pure alethic perfect being theology. Like [P1], [G2] is vacuously satisfied by every necessarily uninstantiated property. We could of course restrict the range of quantification to those things which possibly instantiate the property. But our definition of the $G$-properties would then be a notational variant on our greatness condition [P3], already discussed and rejected in §2.3 above. Or we could restrict the range of the quantification to God. But that would give us a terminological variant of our greatness condition [P5], discussed and rejected in the same section.

If we are going to come up with a genuine alternative to pure perfect being theologies, some more complicated definition of the $G$-properties is needed.

### 4.1.1 Intrinsic goods

As noted above, better-making is a three-place relation between a property, individual, and world. Many of the problems just discussed seem to stem from the fact that whether $F$ is better-making for you depends very much on which thing you are and what world you are in. It is better to have fins than not if you are a shark; not so much if you are a dog.

One way of avoiding some of this variability is to introduce the notion of an intrinsic good. The distinction between intrinsic and extrinsic goods, though, has been explained in two quite different ways. A first way of explaining the distinction says that intrinsic goods are properties whose better-making properties are not dependent on context or external circumstance. Along these lines, Morris says that an intrinsic good

is a property... which endows its bearer with some measure of value, or greatness, or metaphysical stature, regardless of external circumstances. The key idea here is of course that of *intrinsic goodness*. By contrast, *extrinsic goodness* has to do with value determined by external relations or outward circumstances. For example, if there is a sniper on the roof of my office building prepared to shoot anyone who leaves during the next hour, then the property of staying inside this building for more than an hour is a good property or attribute for me to have. But its value clearly depends entirely on external circumstances.[1]

This makes it sound as though intrinsic goods are those properties which are not just better-making, but universally better-making, where that notion can be defined as follows:

*F* is *universally better-making* iff $\forall x \forall w$ (*x* is *F* in *w* $\rightarrow$ *F* is better-making for *x* in *w*)

This would seem to capture the idea of a property which is good to have, no matter what external relations or external circumstances one stands in. Could we define the *G*-properties as the universally better-making ones?

The problem is that the claim that a property is universally better-making is very close to the claim that that property satisfies our greatness condition [P3], discussed in §2.3 above. So the attempt to define the *G*-properties as the universally better-making ones, like [P3], founders on the problem of essentially better-making properties. Properties like the property of having a well-functioning circulatory

---

[1] Morris (1991), 35–6.

system seem to be universally better-making, but are not plausible candidates to be divine attributes. Hence this attempt to define the G-properties fails our adequacy condition.

Fortunately, there is a second, non-equivalent way in which the notion of an intrinsic good can be, and sometimes is, explained. So for example Murray and Rea say that

> there are two broad types of goodness: intrinsic and extrinsic. An object or property is extrinsically good if that object or property is instrumental for bringing about something else that is good. For example, being tall is good for a basketball player because it allows him to shoot unhindered, rebound, and so on. There is nothing about being tall that is good all by itself. . . . But not all goods are merely extrinsic. At some point, extrinsically good things must be good because they bring about something which is just good in itself. Earning a living is good because it is instrumental to, perhaps, being happy. And why is being happy a good thing? One might think that there is no answer to this question: being happy isn't good because it allows us to secure something else; happiness is good just all on its own. That's it. Goods of that sort are intrinsic goods.[2]

This is a plausible line of thought: some things are good for objects only because they bring about some other thing which is also good for those objects; but other properties are just good for objects 'all on their own.' One might then plausibly suggest that we can understand the G-properties in terms of this sort of distinction between intrinsic and extrinsic goods.[3]

The core notion is evidently the notion of one property being better-making for an object in a world because some other property is better-making for that object in that world. So let's say that

$F$ is the *parent* of $G$ relative to $x$, $w$ iff

  (i)  $F$ is better-making for $x$ in $w$,
 (ii)  $G$ is better-making for $x$ in $w$, and
(iii)  (ii) is true because (i) is true

I will use *ancestor* for the transitive closure of the 'parent of' relation.

---

[2] Murray and Rea (2008), 9.
[3] This view is adopted in Morris (1991), Murray and Rea (2008), and Nagasawa (2013).

We can then make precise the thought expressed in the quote from Murray and Rea by saying that

$F$ is an *intrinsic good* for $x$ in $w$ iff

  (i) $F$ is better-making for $x$ in $w$ and
  (ii) $F$ has no ancestors relative to $x$, $w$

And we might then try the following definition of the $G$-properties:

[G3]  $F$ is a $G$-property if $\exists x \exists w$ ($F$ is an intrinsic good for $x$ in $w$)

Let's first ask whether this definition of $G$-properties satisfies [Plausibility].[4]

Given the fact that it is often assumed, more or less without argument, that the greatest possible being would have all intrinsic goods, one would think that it does. But in fact the claim that God has every intrinsic good (in the above sense) is, even given the truth of the claim that God is the greatest possible being, a highly speculative one. One reason is that the following appears to be a coherent and not-implausible view:

Many of the things which are good for human beings are good for us only due to our limitations; these would not be properties which would be good for God to have (and indeed presumably are properties which it is not even possible for God to have). But some of these are not mere instrumental goods. That is, some properties are good for us without being disposed to bring about some other good in us but, for all that, only good for limited beings like us.

The point here is just that the following distinctions appear to be independent:

  • The distinction between properties which are only good for limited creatures like human beings in virtue of their having those limitations, and those which would be good for any being

---

[4] It is worth keeping in mind that some property $F$ can be an intrinsic good of a thing while it is also the case that $F$ brings about some other good for that thing. The key point is just that $F$'s being a good for that thing does not depend on its leading to the other good. Thanks to Evan Fales for helpful discussion here.

- The distinction between properties which are good for a thing only in virtue of bringing about some other good for a thing, and those which are not

The defender of the bridge principle corresponding to [G3] supposes that these distinctions coincide. But there seems to be no obvious reason why this should be so. It is thus at least reasonable to ask the proponent of [G3] why we should have any confidence in the claim that the intrinsic/extrinsic distinction should be any sort of guide to the divine attributes.

Indeed, something stronger can be said. Another way to put the point just made is that the bridge principle corresponding to [G3] is equivalent to the claim that any better-making property of anything has an ancestor which is a property of God. (If this were not true, then there would be an intrinsic good of something which was not a property of God, which would falsify [G3].) But this appears to be extremely implausible.

Consider, to take a simple example, the tulip that I just planted in my yard. It is a better-making property of the tulip that its bulb is about 6 inches under the surface of the soil. This is plausibly an extrinsic good; this is good for the tulip (in part) because it is good for the tulip to survive winter frosts. This is also plausibly an extrinsic good; it is good for the tulip because (maybe) it is good for the tulip to survive many years, or produce more new tulips, or whatever. But it is very obscure how we are ever going to get from this—as we must—to some ancestor of a property of the tulip which is the sort of thing we want to turn up on our list of divine attributes. This strongly suggests that [G3] will fail our [Adequacy] condition.

Similar problems arise when we think about the intrinsic goods of persons. For consider the property of being able to do evil. Most (at least most advocates of the free will defense) consider this a better-making property of persons. Is it an intrinsic good or not? If it is, then [G3] entails, contra the doctrine that God is essentially perfectly good, that God is able to do evil. If it is not, then there must be some ancestor of this property—some property $F$ of mine which is such that it is good for me to do evil because it is good for me to be *F*—which God also possesses. But what is it? This seems like a difficult question to answer.

These problems suggest that [G3] does not do a very good job of capturing the core thought of perfect being theologians who appeal to the distinction between intrinsic and extrinsic goods. And indeed if we look at what such theorists say, they typically do not say that simply God has *every* intrinsically good property, but rather say things like

God has the greatest possible array of great-making properties.[5]

where 'great-making properties' are the intrinsically good ones.

This offers a solution to the problem posed by the tulip. For now we can just grant that there is some ancestor *A* of the property of having its bulb six inches below the surface of the soil which is both an intrinsic good of the tulip and yet not a divine attribute. The reason why is that there are other intrinsic goods which are incompatible with *A* which are such that a being with these attributes would be greater than any being which instantiated *A*. For example, perhaps the relevant property of the tulip could only be had by a material thing, and there could be an immaterial thing which is greater than any material thing.

This suggests that we should add an extra condition to [G3], giving us

*F* is a *G*-property if ($\exists x \exists w$ (*F* is an intrinsic good for *x* in *w*) & *F* is a member of the greatest possible array of intrinsic goods)

Since the first conjunct of the right-hand side is redundant, this simplifies to

[G4]   *F* is a *G*-property if *F* is a member of the greatest possible array of intrinsic goods

This not only solves the problem of the tulip; it also makes our bridge principle much more plausible than the more ambitious [G3]. For now our bridge principle just says that the greatest possible being has the greatest possible array of intrinsic goods. And this is surely quite

---

[5]  Morris (1987), 35; see also Murray and Rea (2008), 8.

plausible; it would be surprising if extrinsic goods could somehow outweigh intrinsic ones, so that something could be greater than the thing with the greatest possible array of intrinsic goods.

However, another way of saying that our bridge principle is quite plausible is to say that it is quite weak. And this is another way of saying that the present version of impure perfect being theology is very close to a pure alethic perfect being theology. Given this, it is perhaps no surprise that [G4] lands us right back in the problems that we encountered when trying to formulate a pure alethic perfect being theology.

It is easy enough to see how we can find properties which satisfy [G3]. We find properties of things which are both good for those things, and are such that they are not good for those things in virtue of some other property being good for them. But how are we to tell whether a given property satisfies [G4]? The natural answer is that we can ask, for a given intrinsic good, whether everything with that property is greater than everything without it. But this is just to ask of such a property whether it satisfies our greatness condition [P2]. And, as we have already seen, the problem of trumping makes it very hard to see how any simple property could satisfy this condition. We are then faced with the same unappetizing menu of options we faced in our discussion of [P2]. We could pursue the restriction strategy, which ends up either foundering on the problem of essentially better-making properties or collapsing into the vacuous [P5]. Or we could pursue the conjunction strategy, which faces the array of problems discussed in §2.4. In either case, the appeal to intrinsic goods will have offered us no advance over pure alethic perfect being theology.

### 4.1.2 Categories of intrinsic goods

There is, however, another move that can be made here, which is suggested by the way that theorists who employ the intrinsic/extrinsic distinction in this context sometimes write. On this way of proceeding, the key claim is not the very strong claim that God possesses every intrinsic good, or the very weak claim that God possesses the greatest possible array of intrinsic goods. Instead, we begin with the thought that every intrinsic good belongs to a certain category of intrinsic goods, which can be ordered on a scale of greatness. The key claim is then that for every such category of intrinsic good, God possesses the greatest member of that category.[6]

One might say, then, that when we examine the intrinsic goods of the sorts of entities with which we are acquainted, what we find are properties had to a certain *degree*. We find, for example, the property of knowing certain things, or being good in certain respects, or having certain powers. Noting this, we might define the following notion:

> D is an *intrinsically good determinable* iff each of its determinates is an intrinsic good of whatever instantiates it.

One might then try to define the G-properties in terms of the notion of an intrinsically good determinable as follows:

> [G5]   F is a G-property if F is a member of the greatest possible array of properties to contain at least one member of every intrinsically good determinable.

The idea behind this suggestion would be to try to come up with a definition of the G-properties which is more informative than [G4] but which does not lead to the sort of counterexamples that render [G3] inadequate. It does the first by requiring that, for every intrinsic property F which anything has, God must have some property which is a determinate of the same determinable as F. It does the second by requiring, not that God have some property of the tulip, but only some property which is a determinate of the same determinable as a property of the tulip.

In the end, though, I think that [G5] just combines the vices of the two approaches tried so far.

As with [G3], [G5] does not fare especially well with [Plausibility]. This is because there seems to be no obvious reason why there could not be an intrinsic good of some being which is so distant from the properties of God that God has no property which is a determinate of

---

[6] This has some affinities with the method of Hill (2004).

the same determinable. This sort of situation need not, of course, conflict with the claim that God is the greatest possible being, since God's greatness could be such as to make possession of any determinate of the relevant determinable simply impossible.

Also as with [G3], [G5] seems to be open to counterexample, and hence fail [Adequacy]. For just as it is hard to see what intrinsic good of the tulip could be a divine attribute, so it is hard to see what determinable the relevant intrinsic good could be a determinate of such that God instantiates some other determinate of that determinable.

And, as with [G4], [G5] seems to do poorly with [Informativeness]. For suppose that we obtain the result that having knowledge to a certain degree is an intrinsically good determinable. That tells us that God must instantiate some determinate of this; but which one? To answer this question, we could ask, of various determinates of this determinable, whether anything with the relevant determinate is greater than anything with any other constellation of determinates of the intrinsically good determinables. But, as with [P2], the problem of trumping makes it hard to see how any determinate of an intrinsically good determinable could pass this test. One may then appeal to the restriction or conjunctive strategies; but again we appear to have made no advance over the pure alethic perfect being theologian.

The last two objections suggest that there is a kind of dilemma here. On the one hand, we might restrict our consideration to very narrow determinables—for example, degrees of physical beauty. That would make the problem posed by the tulip especially difficult, and [Adequacy] especially hard to satisfy. On the other hand, we might help ourselves to extremely broad determinables—for example, degrees of positive aesthetic properties of any kind whatsoever. This makes it easier to satisfy [Adequacy], but exacerbates the difficulty of satisfying [Informativeness].

Summing up: theorists have found it attractive to appeal to the notion of an intrinsic good because the claim that the greatest possible being would have at least many intrinsic goods is quite plausible, and it seems quite plausible that we are able to identify some properties of objects with which we are acquainted as intrinsic goods. What we have seen is that, plausible as these thoughts are, there is no obvious way to use them to derive anything of interest about the attributes of God.

## 4.2 Kind-relative goods

Let's now turn to the second main style of constructing an impure perfect being theology mentioned at the outset: one which appeals, not to various sorts of absolute goods, but rather to goodness relative to a kind. This might seem tailor-made to help with the problems encountered above. For it does seem that we can know, of various kinds, what would make something a better or worse instance of that kind. If we can then identify God as a member of some such kind, it seems that we would then be in a position to ascribe to God the properties which would make something a better instance of that kind.

There is one point about this line of argument which is worth flagging. From the claim that God belongs to some kind $K$, the claim that something is a better $K$ than not if it has some property $F$, and the claim that God is the greatest possible being, it does not follow immediately that God is $F$. After all, something might be the greatest possible being, be of kind $K$, and yet not be maximally great for a $K$—just as something can be the greatest possible human being, and be a basketball player, without being the greatest possible basketball player. Strictly, then, what we'll need is not just the claim that God is the greatest possible being and a member of $K$, but that God is the greatest possible $K$—that God is maximally great *for a K*.[7]

Given this, the definition of the $G$-properties given by a proponent of the kind-relative strategy will be some version of

[G6]   $F$ is a $G$-property if $F$ is a property of the thing which is as great-for-a-$K$ as it is possible to be.

---

[7] This explains why the present approach is not just a version of the restriction strategy, discussed in §2.3 above. Restricting attention to the $K$'s and asking which among them is best is not the same as asking which thing is the greatest $K$.

Some theorists working in the tradition of perfect being theology seem to have some condition on the divine attributes of this general sort in mind. An obvious question for proponents of this strategy is which kind, or kinds, are the operative ones.

One strategy is to work with a very general kind. This is the strategy pursued by Hoffman and Rosenkrantz in *The Divine Attributes*. There they suggest that 'the category relevant to the assessment of God's greatness' is 'the category of Entity,' which is the '*summum genus*, or most general kind, of all categories.'[8] For this suggestion to be useful, we need to be able to figure out what properties would make things better as entities. But this is not altogether easy to do.

Think about how we figure out which things are good-making relative to the kind dog—the properties which make things better dogs. We begin with a pretty clear conception of what dogs are, and what they need to be like to make their way in the world; and we think of as good-making those properties which will enable them to live successful doggy lives. But this sort of method only works because the category of dogs has some substantial unity to it: dogs have a lot in common with each other. The category of entity, by contrast, is the broadest possible category; when I think about my cup of coffee, my daughter, and the set of all squirrels it is just not at all obvious that they have enough in common for me to get any idea of what would make them better members of a category to which they all belong.

Fortunately, Hoffmann and Rosenkrantz tell us what properties are good-making relative to the kind entity:

Since entity is not a category of humanly created artifact, the great-making qualities relevant to the category do not pertain to the sort of function or purpose had by an artifact. Rather, the relevant great-making qualities pertain to an entity's *worthiness for worship and moral admiration.*[9]

I don't disagree with Hoffmann's and Rosenkrantz's claim that God has the qualities which make God worthy for worship and moral admiration; but I am baffled as to how they arrived at that conclusion.

---

[8] Hoffman and Rosenkrantz (2008), 14.
[9] Hoffman and Rosenkrantz (2008), 15–16. Emphasis in the original.

How do we get from the premise that the kind 'entity' is not an artifact kind to the conclusion that things are better entities insofar as they are worthy for worship and moral admiration? The kind 'mushroom' is not an artifact kind; but things are not better mushrooms insofar as they are worthy for worship and moral admiration.

I doubt that Hoffmann and Rosenkrantz really think that it follows from the fact that something is not an artifact kind that something is a better instance of that kind insofar as it is worthy for worship and moral admiration. But then no real attempt is being made to derive the claim that God has the properties which make a thing worthy for worship and moral admiration from the conception of God as the greatest possible member of the kind 'entity'; rather, we're simply importing our assumptions that God is maximally worthy of worship and moral admiration and taking those, rather than any sort of claim about God's being the greatest possible entity, as our starting point. This is perhaps a fine thing to do; but it seems to me at best misleading to present it as in some sense the consequence of the claim that God is the greatest-for-an-entity being.[10]

There is a sense in which the approach suggested by Hoffmann and Rosenkrantz is a notational variant of a pure alethic perfect being theology. The claim that God is the greatest-for-an-entity being, after all, seems very close to the claim that God is the greatest possible being. So if we really tried to plug the kind 'entity' into [G6] and derive the properties of God from there—rather than just importing assumptions about moral admirability and worship-worthiness—it seems likely that we would just encounter the problems of Chapter 2 anew.

---

[10] Nor, I should add, is it perfectly clear, even if we grant the claim that God has those properties which would make God maximally worthy of worship and moral admiration, how to discern which properties make one more worthy for worship. Hoffmann and Rosenkrantz say, for instance, that necessary existence is a property which makes a being more worthy for worship. But again I worry that this is just a matter of importing our assumptions about God while pretending to have derived them in some principled way. Suppose that the number 17 exists necessarily; does this fact make it more worthy of worship than it would otherwise be?

To get a version of the kind-relative view which is substantially different from a pure alethic perfect being theology, we need to start with some kind more substantial and less general than 'entity.' This is the strategy pursued by Brian Leftow. While we saw above that some of his discussions of perfect being methodology have some affinities with a pure alethic perfect being theology which employs [P5] as its greatness condition, his fuller expressions of his views make clear that he has kind-relative goods in mind. Contrasting his approach with a 'pure *a priori*' one, he writes that his style of

argument deals in G-relative goodness, whatever G is. It takes as given that God is G. It tries only to fill out *how* He is G. So our knowledge of the good-making features for Gs guides us. This sort of argument is part of what I call Scriptural perfect being theology, or SPBT. SPBT starts from the conception of God given in Scripture, and uses perfect-being thinking merely to flesh it out. SPBT starts with a skeleton concept of God, and that provides concrete values for G: a person, a knower, etc. We have decent intuitions about what makes for a better person, knower, etc., and SPBT calls only on these.... In SPBT, it is not illicit to assume knowledge of the divine nature. Rather, we accept that from Scripture. The only question is whether God belongs to two kinds, *knower* and *person*, whose highest-degree good-making properties are not compatible. If what is good for a knower as such isn't good for a person as such, then perhaps being a perfect knower isn't compatible with being a perfect person, and one just has to figure out what's most important.[11]

Leftow is surely right that we have reasonable intuitions about what makes something better as a person or as a knower. Can we use these intuitions to derive the attributes of God in a way which will improve on the method of the pure perfect being theologian?

One limitation of this suggestion is obvious: it does not give us a way to derive substantial claims like the claim that God is a person and that God is a knower. These are results which many hope to use perfect being reasoning to deliver; but, on the present model, they are inputs into the system rather than the outputs of perfect being reasoning. This is of course something about which Leftow is quite explicit; but it

---

[11] Leftow (2015), 424.

is an important limitation on the ambitions of perfect being theology as he understands it.

Two other problems are both more significant and more closely connected to the problems that arose in Chapter 2 for pure versions of alethic perfect being theology. Consider Leftow's claim that God has the 'highest-degree good-making properties' for the kind *person*— that God has, that is, all those properties which would make an entity a greater person to the highest degree possible. God then has some property which meets the following condition: necessarily, if it is instantiated, the thing which instantiates it is a greater person than any other possible thing. Let us call properties which meet this condition $GIP_{person}$ properties. Then Leftow's claim is that God has a $GIP_{person}$ property.

But now recall the discussion in §2.4 of the diversity of $GIP$-properties. The same considerations marshaled there will also show that there is also a great diversity of $GIP_{person}$ properties. But then even if we agree with Leftow that God has some $GIP_{person}$ property or other, this fact alone tells us hardly anything about God. Since the argument is exactly parallel to the one in §2.4, I will not belabor the point. As in §2.4, there are defensive moves for the perfect being theologian to make—mainly, the conjunctive-disjunctive strategy and the conjunctive-elimination strategy. But neither seems more likely to be effective in the present context than in the context of a pure alethic perfect being theology.

The second main problem for Leftow's approach stems from the diversity of kinds to which God belongs. As Leftow concedes, we are not quite licensed, even if we adopt his method, to conclude that God has one of the $GIP_{person}$ properties. For (as he notes) *person* is not the only kind to which, according to revelation, God belongs. *Knower* is another; presumably there are others. Focusing on the kind *knower* for the moment, we can consider properties which meet the following condition: necessarily, if something instantiates the property, then that thing is a greater knower than any other possible thing. Call properties which meet this condition $GIP_{knower}$ properties. The diversity of $GIP$-properties, discussed in §2.4, shows that some $GIP_{person}$ properties are incompossible with some GIP*knower* properties. Given this (as Leftow in effect notes) it is at least conceivable that the possibly instantiated GIP*person* property is incompatible with the possibly instantiated GIP*knower* property. In that case, the greatest possible person will not be the greatest possible knower.

In this situation, Leftow says, 'one just has to figure out what's most important.'[12] By this, I take it he means that 'one just has to figure out whether the greatest possible person is a greater being overall than the greatest possible knower.'

Here is a first pass at the kind of strategy that Leftow seems to have in mind:

Suppose that God belongs to kinds $K_1, K_2 \ldots K_n$. We can then consider, generalizing the sorts of conditions stated above, the notions of a GIP$_{K_1}$ property, a GIP$_{K_2}$ property . . . and a GIP$_{K_n}$ property. Each of these classes of properties will have one possibly instantiated member.[13]

There are then two possibilities. Either (i) there is one possible thing that instantiates each of these, or (ii) there is not.

In case (i), God is that thing, and hence has one of the GIP$_{K_1}$ properties, one of the GIP$_{K_2}$ properties, . . . and one of the GIP$_{K_n}$ properties.

In case (ii), there are a number of distinct possible things, one of which (say) instantiates a GIP$_{K_1}$ property, one of which instantiates a GIP$_{K_2}$ property . . . and one of which instantiates a GIP$_{K_n}$ property. We can then ask, of these things, which is the greatest overall. God is that thing.

However, closer examination suggests this can't be quite right. For consider the possibility that distinct possible things instantiate the various 'greatest-if-possible-for-a-$K$' properties, but that there is some other possible thing which instantiates none of these properties, but

---

[12] Leftow (2015), 424.
[13] Here I'm setting aside ties for simplicity, since they seem irrelevant to the present point.

nonetheless has the greatest overall distribution of the properties which make one 'better-as-a-$K_1$,' 'better-as-a-$K_2$,' etc. Presumably, in that case, that thing is God. Otherwise, God would be less than the greatest possible being overall.

Let's say that a being which has the greatest overall distribution of the 'greatest-if-possible-for-a-$K_x$' properties is the 'greatest-overall-for-a-$K$' being. This suggests that we should revise the foregoing response to case (ii):

In case (ii), there are a number of distinct possible things, one of which instantiates a $\text{GIP}_{K_1}$ property, one of which instantiates a $\text{GIP}_{K_2}$ property... and one of which instantiates a $\text{GIP}_{K_n}$ property. We can then ask what possible thing is the greatest overall-for-a-$K$ being—which being, that is, has the greatest overall distribution of the properties which make things great for a $K_1$, great for a $K_2$,... and great for a $K_n$. God is that thing.

We can then state the starting point for Leftow's method as follows:

Either (a) the greatest possible person is also the greatest possible instance of all of the other kinds to which God belongs or (b) it is not.

If (a), then God is the greatest possible person, and so has one of the $\text{GIP}_{person}$ properties.

If (b), then God may not have one of the $\text{GIP}_{person}$ properties, but is the greatest-overall-for-a-$K$ being.

Given that in case (a) God is also the greatest-overall-for-a-$K$ being, we know that in either case (a) or case (b), God is the greatest-overall-for-a-$K$ being. That is as it should be.

But it is worth emphasizing that, absent argument, we do not know whether the true situation is case (a) or case (b). As mentioned above, it would not be difficult to modify and expand the various examples of GIP-properties discussed in §2.4 to provide examples of, for example, $\text{GIP}_{person}$ properties and $\text{GIP}_{knower}$ properties which are incompatible with each other. Whether we are in case (a) or case (b) thus depends on which $\text{GIP}_{person}$ and $\text{GIP}_{knower}$ properties are possibly instantiated. So to be confident that we can reason from the assumption that we are in case (a), we would have to have independent arguments which told us which GIP$_{person}$ and GIP$_{knower}$ properties are possibly instantiated. But it is hard to see what these arguments could be, if not arguments about the attributes of God—and of course if we had arguments of that sort, we would not need perfect being reasoning.

Given that we do not know whether we are in situation (a) or (b), Leftow's account of the G-properties is equivalent to the following:

[G7]   F is a G-property if F is a property of the greatest-overall-for-a-K being

And now we face a too-familiar problem: how do we tell whether a given property is a property of the greatest-overall-for-a-K being? Here the problem of trumping arises, just as it did for the pure perfect being theologian; and the twin strategies—the restriction strategy and the conjunctive strategy—are as problematic as before.

This is no accident. The fact that Leftow's starting point reduces to the view that the G-properties can be defined as in [G7] shows that, while his method can be presented in a way which sounds quite different from a pure perfect being theology—the 'pure *a priori*' method from which he distances himself—under pressure it collapses into a view which is barely distinct from pure perfect being theology.

Indeed, given a plausible assumption, it is not distinct at all. It is after all very plausible that, necessarily, something is the greatest possible being iff it is a property of the greatest-overall-for-a-K being. For this to be false there would have to be a being which exceeds the greatness of a being with the greatest overall blend of properties which make for a greater instance of *every kind to which God belongs*. It is hard to see how this could be so. What extra good would such a being have, which is not a kind-relative good for any kind at all to which God belongs? But of course if we assume that, necessarily, something is the greatest-overall-for-a-K being iff it is the greatest possible being, then Leftow's approach to perfect being theology is just a notational variant of pure alethic perfect being theology.

And this suggests a more general result. The only part of Leftow's theory that was used to generate the collapse toward a pure perfect being theology was the assumption that we should employ multiple kind-relative goods—at least the kinds *person* and *knower*—in determining the properties of God. This can be used to state a dilemma for the kind-relative approach. Either we use a single kind-relative good, or multiple-kinds. The former approach is difficult to sustain, since we either choose very broad but uninformative kinds (like *entity*) or potentially informative kinds (like *person*) which, alone, threaten to give us a one-sided view of God. The latter approach opens up the possibility of conflict between the kind-relative goods, which begins the slide toward [G7] and, ultimately, a pure alethic perfect being theology.

# 5

# Conflict and the Problem of Hidden Attributes

In the preceding three chapters, I've discussed the problems that arise for various specific versions of perfect being theology. The aim of this chapter is to introduce a more general problem for the constructive program of perfect being theology, one which seems to arise for any way of deriving the attributes from the modal conception of God.

Because the problem is closely related to one raised by Duns Scotus, I'll start by briefly discussing a criticism of perfect being reasoning which he considers. It begins with the following point:

> Every unqualified perfection, to the highest degree, is necessarily in the highest nature. An unqualified perfection is said to be that which is *better in anything than what is not it.* . . . If however, it is understood not only in itself and in anything if it can be in it, but unqualifiedly in anything, then it is false. For wisdom is not better [than non-wisdom] in a dog, for nothing is good for that thing which it contradicts.[1]

Scotus' claim that 'nothing is good for that thing which it contradicts' seems, intuitively, quite plausible; if being $F$ is incompatible with my existence, it is difficult to see how it could be better for me to be $F$ than not $F$.

At first glance, it might be hard to see how this could pose a problem for the perfect being theologian. After all, even if being wise is not

---

[1] Scotus, *De Primo Principio*, 4. n. 3. Translation in Cross (2005), 50–1. In what follows I am indebted to Cross' excellent discussion of Scotus' views of 'perfect being' reasoning.

better for a dog than being not wise, it still might be the case that everything which is wise is better than any possible thing which is not wise—and that seems like enough to get us the wanted result that the greatest possible being must be wise.[2]

But the problem, Scotus thinks, is that—given that nothing is good for that thing which it contradicts—it is hard to see how we could know that everything wise is better than *any* possible thing which lacks wisdom:

> If you take wisdom denominatively, it is better than any incompossible denominative, and yet you still have not proved that the first being is wise. I say you beg the question. You can only have that something wise is better than something not wise, excluding the first being.[3]

On Richard Cross' reading of these passages, Scotus is identifying a kind of circularity in the perfect being theologian's reasoning:

> he does not see that we can know that wise things are better than things possessing a property incompatible with being wise unless we already know that the first being is wise. For if it should turn out that the first being is not wise, then wisdom would not be a pure perfection. The opponent, then, begs the question, for the claim that wisdom is a pure perfection can be made only by inference from the fact that the first being is wise; but this last claim—that the first being is wise—is precisely what the opponent is trying to prove.[4]

The argument seems to run as follows: suppose that God's nature is inconsistent with God being wise, and so that God is not wise. Then wisdom is not a property of the greatest possible being. This follows from the fact that God is the greatest possible being, since, given this, it follows from God's lacking wisdom that there is some being—namely God—which lacks wisdom and yet is greater than anything which has wisdom. Hence the perfect being theologian had better be in a position to rule out the hypothesis that God is not wise. But if the perfect being theologian were in a position to rule out this hypothesis,

---

[2] Here I set aside the problems with this kind of reasoning, for example the problem of trumping, detailed in the preceding chapters.

[3] Scotus, *De Primo Principio*, 4. n. 3. Translation in Cross (2005), 52.

[4] Cross (2005), 52.

she would already have an argument for the very proposition—that God is wise—for which she hoped to use perfect being reasoning to argue.

The perfect being theologian is likely to object that this reasoning is a bit too quick, since a version of it would seem to show that any argument for any conclusion must be circular. Imagine that philosopher X wants to argue for some proposition $p$. One could run a version of the Scotus/Cross objection as follows:

Suppose that $\neg p$ is true. This entails that at least one of the premises of X's argument for $p$ must be false. (At least, it entails this if X's argument is valid.) So X must be in a position to rule out the truth of $\neg p$. But if X could do this, then X must already have an argument for the conclusion—$p$—for which X hoped to argue.

This kind of objection cannot in general be a good one; simply pointing out that the negation of the conclusion of an argument entails the falsity of one of its premises does not show that the argument is, in any objectionable sense, question-begging.

While this reply to the Scotus/Cross argument is correct as far as it goes, I think that it does not show that the argument fails. While it is true that valid arguments are not, just in virtue of being valid, question-begging, there is reason to think that Scotus' objection nonetheless sticks. The reason is just that, for any attribute that seems to be a plausible candidate to be a property of the greatest possible being, there are special reasons to think that we should have a relatively low credence in the claim that that attribute is compossible with God's nature. That, at least, is what I will try to argue in the remainder of this chapter.

The argument begins with an observation of which perfect being theologians are very much aware: it is at least epistemically possible that some initially plausible candidates to be divine attributes conflict with others, so that it is impossible for a single entity to possess both. Examples of at least apparent conflicts of this sort are well-known:

- It is plausible that God's creation of other beings was free. But free action entails the possibility of having done otherwise. So,

God could have not created any other beings. But it is better for there to be beings distinct from God than for there not to be. So, God could have done less than the best thing. So, God does not have [□G].[5]

- It is good that there be beings other than God with free will. So, God created beings with free will. There are truths about what those beings will freely do in the future—e.g., the truth that Bob will freely eat a hamburger in 2029. If God has [□K], then God in 2016 believes that Bob freely will eat a hamburger in 2029. In 2029, Bob will have no choice about what God believed in 2016. Further, since God cannot be mistaken, it is a necessary truth that if God now believes that Bob will freely eat a hamburger in 2029, Bob will. Since Bob has no choice about necessary truths, he has no choice about whether this conditional is true. But if someone has no choice about whether $p$ is true, and no choice about whether it is true that if $p$, then $q$, then they have no choice about whether $q$ is true. So, Bob in 2029 has no choice about whether he will eat a hamburger. But that contradicts our supposition. So, God does not now know that Bob will eat a hamburger in 2029, and God does not have [□K].[6]
- God has [□G]. So, it is impossible for God to do anything that is morally wrong. But I can do things that are morally wrong. So, I have a power that God does not have. So, God is not omnipotent.[7]

We could go on. Each of the arguments just informally sketched is, of course, very controversial. But I think that they make plausible the thought that two properties could both seem like very plausible candidates to be properties of the greatest possible being, and yet be incompossible.

---

[5] See, among many other places, Flint (1983) and Rowe (2004). An alternative version of this kind of argument focuses on God's responsibility, or praiseworthiness, rather than divine freedom. See, for discussion, Morriston (1985) and Bergmann and Cover (2006).

[6] See, among many other places, van Inwagen (2008).

[7] The locus classicus here is Pike (1969); see also Morriston (2001).

A second, related possibility—relevant only to adherents of some revealed religion—is that properties which seem to satisfy one's chosen greatness condition might conflict with the content of revealed doctrine about God. For example, it has seemed to many that immutability is a property which the greatest possible being would have. (Indeed, that is the conclusion of one of the earliest perfect being arguments, in *Republic* II.) But that view at least apparently conflicts with the Christian doctrine that God became human, which certainly seems to involve change of some sort. As above, any case of this sort is bound to be controversial; but such cases illustrate a possibility to which the perfect being theologian should be open.

How should the perfect being theologian respond to the fact that a property may seem to be one which would be a property of the greatest possible being, but also be incompossible with either other properties that seem to meet this condition or properties attributed to God by revelation? Brian Leftow gives what I think would be a fairly standard answer:

If being F is incompatible with some divine attribute initially given by Scripture, this *prima facie* claim is overruled. If being F is compatible with all scriptural 'givens' and with all other outputs of this 'first stage' procedure, then *ultima facie* and *simpliciter*, God is F. If being F is compatible with all Scriptural 'givens' but incompatible with some first-stage output H, then if having F and the rest of these is better than having H and the rest, *ultima facie* God has just F. If F and H (plus the rest of the given divine nature) are equal or incommensurable, *ultima facie* God is H or F, but 'perfect being' reasoning does not permit us to choose between them.[8]

Surely, as Leftow says, whether a property really does satisfy our chosen greatness condition is a defeasible matter, about which we can be mistaken. Leftow notes two ways in which we can learn that an initial impression that a property satisfies a greatness condition is mistaken. One is that some other property, incompossible with the first, can be attributed to God by revelation. The second is that some

---

[8] Leftow (2012), 10.

other property, incompossible with the first, can also seem to satisfy that greatness condition.

If and when such conflicts occur, Leftow suggests what seems at first to be a very sensible strategy. The idea is that we use the method of perfect being theology to arrive at an initial list of candidates for the attributes; but we arrive at our considered view of the divine attributes only after a kind of consistency check of those candidates with revealed doctrine about God, and with each other. In the case of the first sort of conflict, he suggests abandoning the property which seems to satisfy our greatness condition in favor of the property attributed to God by revelation. In the case of the second sort of conflict, we simply ask which of the two incompossible properties—in conjunction with the other properties we attribute to God—would make God greater, and then attribute that one to God.

Sensible as this strategy sounds, I think that it dramatically underestimates the problem posed by the possibility of conflict for the method of perfect being theology. One does not have to be an apophatic theologian to concede that God has attributes which are beyond our comprehension. Call these God's *hidden attributes*. Let's call, by contrast, those properties of God which are given to us either by revelation or perfect being reasoning God's *visible attributes*.

The reasonable view, I think, is that the former vastly exceed the latter. On any traditional conception of divine transcendence, our understanding of God is not just partial, but radically incomplete and defective. As Robert Adams nicely puts it, 'God's superiority exceeds our cognitive grasp in a positive direction, and is not exhausted by negative or universalizing options on properties familiar to us.'[9] So let's suppose that this is true. Why should this matter to the perfect being theologian?

The first point made above was that something can seem to satisfy a greatness condition, but in the end conflict with one or more of God's visible attributes. When a property $F$ seems to satisfy a greatness condition, then, we should have some initial nonzero credence $n$ in

---

[9] Adams (1999), 52.

the proposition that $F$ conflicts with a visible attribute. This credence might then go up or down as we do the sort of consistency check with other visible attributes described above.

Presumably, then, we should also have some nonzero credence $m$ in the proposition that $F$ conflicts with a hidden attribute. While it is difficult to say what $m$ should be in any precise way, the following three points suggest that $m$ should be quite high:

- As the above examples illustrate, there are a fair number of at least prima facie conflicts between properties which seem to satisfy our greatness condition and visible properties of God. This is so despite the fact that our list of visible attributes is pretty sparse. This suggests that $n$ should be reasonably high.
- If the hidden attributes of God greatly exceed the visible ones, and if the odds of a given hidden attribute leading to conflict are not less than the odds of a given visible attribute leading to conflict, then $m$ should be much higher than $n$.
- There is no reason to believe that the odds of a given hidden attribute leading to conflict are less than the odds of a given visible attribute leading to conflict. Indeed, given that the former are more distant from our understanding, it is perhaps more likely that they would conflict with our initial judgements about what the greatest possible being would be like.

The conclusion of this line of argument is that we should have a fairly high credence that any attribute which seems to us like a plausible candidate to be a property of the greatest possible being is incompossible with some hidden attribute of God.

This is not an attack on a straw man. We can grant that, as Rea says, 'it is no part of perfect being theology to suppose that [its] method is perfectly reliable, or that intuitions about perfection are evidentially superior to or even on a par with the claims of scripture as evidence about what God is like.'[10] The present argument is not just a reassertion of this correct point; it is an argument for the

---

[10] Rea (2016), 218.

conclusion that the possibility of conflict, plus the reality of hidden divine attributes, shows that we should have very low confidence in our intuitions about which properties are properties of the greatest possible being.

In the case of possible conflict with visible attributes, we can increase our confidence in there being no real conflict via a consistency check of the sort discussed above. But of course in the case of conflict with hidden attributes, there is no such possibility. So, if our initial credence in the absence of conflict should be quite low, there seems little hope of improving matters with further reflection.

Just how serious this worry is depends on just how low our confidence in the absence of conflict should be. But at least some traditional views of the relationship between the visible and hidden attributes of God suggest that it should be quite low indeed. Aquinas, for example, writes

But God, whose being is infinite . . . is infinitely knowable. Now no created intellect can know God infinitely. For the created intellect knows the Divine essence more or less perfectly in proportion as it receives a greater or lesser light of glory. Since therefore the created light of glory received into any created intellect cannot be infinite, it is clearly impossible for any created intellect to know God in an infinite degree. Hence it is impossible that it should comprehend God.[11]

If the relationship between the hidden and the visible attributes of God is a relationship of infinite to finite, then the problem posed by the possibility of conflict seems very serious. Seen in this light, it is not unreasonable to wonder whether perfect being theology rests on an unjustified confidence in our ability to comprehend the divine nature.[12]

---

[11] *Summa Theologica* Ia.12.a7.

[12] There is a connection here with the 'skeptical theist' response to the argument from evil, which argues (roughly) that we should expect to be ignorant of the facts which explain the existence of certain evils. Given this, our inability to explain these evils is not evidence (or not much evidence) against the existence of God. One might base this position on ignorance of various sorts. Sometimes, as in van Inwagen (1991), it is ignorance about modality and value. But other times it appears to be based at least in part on our ignorance of the nature of God. This sort of skeptical theism would seem

This is obviously a form of skeptical argument. And, as with other skeptical arguments, one might worry that the present argument over-generalizes to an implausible skepticism about matters of fact about which we plausibly do have knowledge. So, for example, consider the following skeptical argument:

Call the facts about the universe which we know the visible facts, and the facts about the universe which we do not know the invisible facts. Now, we are all familiar with the phenomenon of coming across some claim which seems true, but which turns out to conflict with something we know. So, for any claim which seems true, we should have some nonzero credence that it will conflict with something we know. But presumably the hidden facts about the universe greatly outnumber the visible facts; so we should have a higher credence that something which seems true conflicts with some hidden fact. And, the hidden facts being further removed from our knowledge of the world, there is perhaps an even greater chance that they would conflict with something which seems true to us; and so our credence that any given claim which seems true to us conflicts with some hidden fact should be quite high. So, we should not believe any new claims which seem true to us.[13]

This argument has a false conclusion; so it must either be invalid, or have a false premise. But it seems to be of the same form as our argument from hidden properties, and the premises of one argument seem parallel to those of the other. So why doesn't the unsoundness of this skeptical argument show that the argument from hidden properties is similarly unsound?

My answer to this question is predictable: for any domain of belief about which skepticism is not appropriate, beliefs in that domain are not analogous to beliefs about the properties of the greatest possible being.

Let's consider first the relatively simple case of perceptual judgements. It is simply not the case that our perceptual judgements frequently come into conflict with other things we know about the world on the basis of perceptual experience. Now, it does occasionally

to be at least in tension with the optimism about our knowledge of God embodied by the project of perfect being theology.

[13] Thanks to Brian Cutter for raising the objection in this form.

happen, as in the case of certain sorts of illusions, but it is a very rare kind of event. So, for any given perceptual judgement, our credence in the proposition that that judgement conflicts with something else we do or will know about the world on the basis of perceptual experience should be extremely low. This contrasts with the case of beliefs about God, where apparent visible attributes of God quite frequently conflict with other apparent visible attributes.

How about conflict between our perceptual judgements and hidden facts about the universe? It is of course true that there are hidden facts about the universe; but is there any reason to think that conflict between our perceptual judgements and hidden features of the universe is more likely than conflict between our perceptual judgements and things we know about (i.e., visible facts about) the universe?

To answer this question, it is useful to compare two views of the relationship between, to use the terms of Sellars (1962), the scientific and the manifest image of the world. A familiar question is whether scientific findings—which reveal previously hidden attributes of the universe—are inconsistent with commonsense beliefs (which include, paradigmatically, perceptual judgements). However one answers this question, I think, we can see that there is little reason to think that the present objection to perfect being theology leads to an implausible skepticism about perceptual judgements.

Consider first the view that the manifest and scientific images do not conflict; scientific findings about the physical world are not inconsistent with our perceptual judgements about the colors, shapes, and other qualities of things in our environment. On this view, I think that there is little reason to think that we should have a very high credence in the claim that there are conflicts between our perceptual judgements and hidden features of the world. If past scientific revelation of formerly hidden features has led to no conflict, why think that there are conflicts between our perceptual judgements and those features of the physical world which remain hidden?

So consider instead the view that the scientific and manifest images are in conflict, and that science has revealed that the physical world does not contain anything with the color properties, shape properties, etc. which are attributed by our experiences to things in the world. If this view is correct, then (by reasoning parallel to that just given) I think that we should have a fairly high credence in the claim that there are conflicts between our perceptual judgements and hidden features of the physical world. And that does, by argument parallel to the argument sketched above against perfect being reasoning about God, lead to skepticism about our perceptual judgements. But that is obviously no problem for the objection to perfect being reasoning, since, if there is a conflict between the scientific image of the world and our ordinary perceptual judgements, skepticism about those judgements is simply appropriate.

This is not, so far, a general response to the worry that the skeptical argument against perfect being reasoning overgenerates; I have only argued that it does not lead to an implausible skepticism about perceptual judgements. (Depending on one's view of the relationship between the manifest and scientific images, it either does not lead to skepticism about perceptual judgements, or it leads to a plausible skepticism.) Are there other domains of belief about which our skeptical argument would lead to an implausible skepticism?

A good candidate here might seem to be beliefs about the truth of scientific theories. Surely, one might think, it is reasonable in many cases for us to believe that a certain scientific theory is true. And yet, in the past, we have consistently found that well-confirmed scientific theories turned out to be inconsistent with facts about the physical world which were previously unknown. Given this, it is reasonable for us now to have a relatively high credence in the claim that our current scientific theories are inconsistent with facts about the physical world which are, at present, hidden. And that seems to, via the same sort of reasoning employed against the perfect being theologian, lead to skepticism about belief in the truth of our best scientific theories.

This is a spin on the familiar 'pessimistic meta-induction' against belief in the truth of present scientific theories. Since many do think that it is reasonable to believe in the truth of our best-supported current theories, it may seem to cast doubt on the form of argument employed against the perfect being theologian. Notably, though, responses to the meta-induction typically do not target the form of argument involved.[14] Rather, the main responses by scientific realists target either the assumption (in the present terms) that there is real conflict between facts about the physical world and past theories which are relevantly similar to present theories or give up the claim that present theories are true simpliciter in favor of some weaker but still substantial claim.[15] By contrast, it is hard to deny the reality of conflict between initially plausible candidates to be properties of the greatest possible being.

I conclude that there is no obvious way to show that the present skeptical doubts about perfect being theology lead to an implausibly sweeping skeptical conclusion. Even setting aside the problems for various versions of perfect being theology belabored in Chapters 2–4, a reasonable modesty about our ability to cognize the greatest possible being suggests that the correct attitude toward the outputs of perfect being reasoning is, not confidence, but, at best, agnosticism.

[14] An exception is the view that the meta-induction involves an instance of the base rate fallacy; see, for example, Lewis (2001). But that objection to the meta-induction doesn't have any obvious analogue in the case of the line of argument developed in this chapter against the perfect being theologian.

[15] An example would be the structuralist view that our best theories correctly describe the relations between entities but perhaps do not correctly characterize the entities so related. If past theories attribute the same structure to the world as our present theories, then the meta-inductive argument against structural realism does not get off the ground. See, for example, Worrall (1989).

# 6

# Permissible Tinkering
# with The Concept of God

So far, our focus has been on the constructive program of perfect being theology: the attempt to use the modal conception of God in the derivation of the divine attributes. I've argued that this constructive program is largely a failure. But the principle that God is the greatest possible being can be put to defensive as well as constructive uses; and even if the constructive program of perfect being theology is a failure, these defensive uses might still be of interest.

These defensive uses of the idea of God as the greatest possible being can be introduced by thinking about the dialectic between the atheist and the theist when assessing arguments against the existence of God. Typically, arguments against the existence of some entity take the form of arguments that nothing has some property $F$—where it is common ground that, if the entity in question did exist, it would be $F$. Arguments against the existence of God are no exception. Typically, they aim to demonstrate that some property typically counted among the divine attributes is not, or could not be, instantiated.

In response to arguments of this form—as well as in response to perceived conflicts between divine attributes—theists often face pressure to give up some pre-theoretically attractive thesis about the divine attributes. In response, theists have two options: they can try to find some flaw in the argument in question, or they can accept its conclusion and simply revise their view of God.

Some examples of the second strategy are well known. One might, for instance, weaken one's view of God's power in response to perceived conflicts with the necessitation of the law of non-contradiction, or with God's essential goodness; and one might weaken one's view of God's knowledge in response to perceived conflicts with the existence of freedom of the will, or with the existence of essentially first-personal propositions.[1] Other examples are not hard to come by.

This is a risky strategy, for one always runs the risk of unacceptably watering down the concept of God. This is a response that undergraduates often have in response to the claim that God cannot bring about contradictions; they are often inclined to hold, for example, that no being which could not make $2 + 2 = 5$ could qualify as God. But this sort of response can't always be dismissed as 'an undergraduate response.' When, for example, the open theist tells us that God does not know what I will do tomorrow, the worry that we have moved too far from the traditional conception of God deserves to at least be taken seriously.

It would be good to have some principled way of thinking about this topic—some principled way of deciding whether a given way of revising our views of the divine attributes is, as Peter van Inwagen nicely puts it, 'permissible tinkering' with the concept of God, and when it is not.[2] Let's say that some pre-theoretically attractive candidate to be among the divine attributes is *dispensable* if a theist can deny that God has that attribute without unacceptably watering down our concept of God, and *mandatory* if not. Then what we seek is a principled way of distinguishing dispensable from mandatory candidates for the divine attributes.

Here it is very natural to—as van Inwagen and others have done—appeal to the principle that God is the greatest possible being. As noted above, this claim is often said to, in some sense, express our concept of God; and, if this is true, it seems as though examination of the notion of a greatest possible being ought to help us figure out when some claim about God conflicts with the core of our conception of God.

[1] See, respectively, (among many other places) Mavrodes (1963) and Flint and Freddoso (1983b); Morris (1983); van Inwagen (2008); and Wierenga (2001).
[2] van Inwagen (2006), 81.

To make this work, we want a formulation of the principle that God is the greatest possible being which could in principle be accepted by atheist and theist alike, and hence could be used to structure debates about the existence of God. [GPB], which trivially entails that God exists, is obviously not well-suited for the task.

Fortunately, there is a familiar way to formulate principles of the sort we want. To illustrate, consider the question of whether the claim that there are witches—which we can call 'Wiccanism'—is true. If we want a debate between Wiccanists and their opponents to be productive, we should want to find some neutral way of formulating the condition which would have to be satisfied for witches to exist. Let us suppose that Wiccanists and non-Wiccanists agree on the claim that for something to be a witch is for that thing to be a woman with evil magical powers—while of course disagreeing over the question of whether anything is a woman with evil magical powers.[3] Then we might formulate the claim on which they agree as the biconditional

[Witch]  There are witches iff there are women with evil magical powers

The debate can then be significantly structured by the content of the right-hand side of the biconditional. For suppose that the anti-Wiccanists provide an argument for the claim that nothing is $F$. The Wiccanist may then reply either by finding a flaw in the argument, or by giving up the claim that witches are $F$. But with a principle like [Witch] in hand, the scope of this second sort of maneuver is constrained in a principled way, for the Wiccanist cannot simply concede that nothing is $F$ if so doing would entail that there are no women with evil magical powers.

Given our interest in finding a parallel constructive way to constrain debates between theists and non-theists, we can formulate a similar biconditional which aims to state the conditions under which God

---

[3] Surprisingly, the *OED* defines 'witch' as 'a woman thought to have evil magic powers' which would make witch trials paradigms of reliability.

would exist. It is natural to use the principle that God is the greatest possible thing to do this, as follows:

[Conditions]   God exists iff $\exists x \, [\forall y : y \neq x] \, \forall w \, (x_\alpha > y_w)$

This says that God exists just in case there is something which is greater than any other thing in any possible world—just in case, that is, the greatest possible being actually exists.[4] It is reasonable to think that, just as [Witch] provides a Wiccanism-neutral account of the conditions under which Wiccanism would be true, so—if the claim that God is the greatest possible being captures the core of our concept of God—[Conditions] provides an account of the conditions under which God exists which should be acceptable to theist and non-theist alike.

If it can, then—as with [Witch]—it appears that we can use [Conditions] to provide the wanted principled distinction between dispensable and mandatory attributes. For suppose that we are considering whether God is $F$. We can ask: would denying that God is $F$—and hence presumably also denying, for attributes of interest, that anything is $F$—entail that there could be a being greater than the greatest actual being? If we answer 'Yes,' then it would seem that $F$ is a mandatory attribute. For then denying that God is $F$ would entail the falsity of the right-hand side of [Conditions], which we are (at present) assuming to state the conditions under which God would exist. If we answer 'No,' on the other hand, then $F$ would seem to be dispensable. For then denying that God is $F$ would be consistent with maintaining that the greatest possible being actually exists, and hence (given [Conditions]) consistent with belief in the existence of God.

We might state the resulting principle as follows:

---

[4] Many proponents of the idea that God is the greatest possible being might also accept this principle if the right-hand side were strengthened to require, not just that $x$ be greater than any other thing in any world, but also to require that $x$ could not be greater than $x$ actually is. Since nothing in what follows hangs on the difference between these two formulations, I stick with the simpler [Conditions] in what follows.

[Dispensable]    If the proposition that God is not *F* does not entail the falsity of the right-hand side of [Conditions], then *F* is dispensable.[5]

[Dispensable] gives us a sufficient condition for a property's being dispensable, which the theist might then deploy in responding to various arguments against the existence of God. I will call the attempt to use [Dispensable] in this way the *perfect being defense*.

It is worth emphasizing that, even if the constructive programs of alethic, epistemic, and impure perfect being theology fail to deliver their intended results, the perfect being defense might still be of use. For even if the principle that God is the greatest possible being cannot deliver substantial positive results about the divine attributes, we might still be able to see that denying that God has certain attributes is consistent with that principle.

Let's now look at a few instances in which theists have put this sort of strategy to work.

## 6.1 The perfect being defense in action

The perfect being defense is more often deployed than explicitly articulated. But one person who makes the sort of strategy just sketched more than usually explicit is Peter van Inwagen. To see the form it takes in his work, let's consider van Inwagen's discussion of omniscience and freedom of the will in Chapter 5 of *The Problem of Evil*. There van Inwagen is imagining an atheist challenging the free will defense on the grounds that free will is incompatible

---

[5] Some delicacy is required in understanding what 'entails' should mean in a thesis of this sort. It cannot simply mean 'necessitates,' since this would, given that most false predications of God will be necessarily false, threaten to trivialize the thesis. The intended interpretation is rather something like 'has as a clear a priori consequence.' I ignore this in what follows, since the objections that I raise against the perfect being defense have nothing to do with the threat of triviality.

with omniscience—and that, necessarily, if God exists, then God is omniscient. Here is what van Inwagen says in reply to the atheist:

Now consider these two propositions:

    (i) X will freely do A at the future moment t
    (ii) Y, a being whose beliefs cannot be mistaken, now believes that X will
        do A at t.

These two propositions are consistent with each other or they are not. If they are consistent, there is no problem of omniscience and freedom. Suppose they are inconsistent. Then it is impossible for a being whose beliefs cannot be mistaken now to believe that someone will at some future moment freely perform some particular action. Hence, if free will exists, it is impossible for any being to be omniscient.... (81)

Let us say that a being is *classically omniscient* iff, for every proposition, that being knows whether that proposition is true. Given that it rules out divine classical omniscience, one might think that the view that (i) and (ii) are inconsistent is itself inconsistent with theism. van Inwagen suggests another option:

why should we not qualify the 'standard' definition of omniscience ... ? Why not say that even an omniscient being is unable to know certain things— those such that its knowing them would be an intrinsically impossible state of affairs.... This qualification of the 'standard' definition of omniscience is in the spirit of what I contended ... were permissible revisions of the properties in our list of divine attributes ... he will possess knowledge in the highest degree that is metaphysically possible, and will therefore not be debarred from the office 'greatest possible being'. (82)

Here van Inwagen seems to be reasoning as follows: if there is a genuine incompatibility between free will and classical omniscience, then having classical omniscience (in a world with free agents) is an impossible property. Hence it is not a property which is such that, were we to deny it to God, this denial would conflict with the proposition that God is the greatest possible being. And if denying a property to God does not conflict with the right-hand side of [Conditions], then [Dispensable] tells us that this property must be (in our terms) a dispensable one. Hence the theist can reasonably deny—if (i) and (ii) really are inconsistent—that God (or anything else) is classically omniscient.

One step in this reasoning deserves slightly closer examination. This is the inference from the claim that

The property of having classical omniscience is impossible.[6]

to

Denying that God is classically omniscient is consistent with the claim that God is the greatest possible being.

One natural way to unpack this reasoning would be as follows. If the property of being classically omniscient is impossible, there is no being in any world which is classically omniscient. But then denying that God is classically omniscient cannot imply that God is not the greatest possible being. For it could do that only if there could be a being which was classically omniscient and, in virtue of possession of this property, greater than God. Since there could be no such being, this possibility is foreclosed.

This is a reasonable line of thought; it does seem that denying God some property could 'debar God from the office "greatest possible being"' only if denying God this property could make some other possible being greater than God. And it does seem that it could have this effect only if there could be some other possible being with the property in question. Since this form of reasoning seems to be general, it appears to be a corollary of [Dispensable] that the following principle is true:

[Impossible]   If $F$ is impossible, then $F$ is dispensable.

This is, as van Inwagen's argumentative strategy makes clear, a useful principle for the theist to have in hand. (One may suspect that it is a bit *too* useful. More on this sort of worry in the next section.)

Other instances of the perfect being defense in action—though typically not as explicit as the example from van Inwagen—are not hard to find. An example—which also focuses on omniscience—can

---

[6] Strictly, the relevant claim is that the conjunction of classical omniscience and coexistence with the existence of distinct free agents is impossible; I ignore this complication for simplicity, since it does not affect the general point at issue.

be found by looking at the debate between Alvin Plantinga and Patrick Grim over the question of whether classical omniscience is possible. Grim defends the position that it is not, on the grounds that Cantorian arguments show that there can be no set of, or quantification over, all true propositions, and that this result is inconsistent with the possibility of a being who knows all true propositions. One of Plantinga's central lines of reply to this argument is to say that

> the problem... is not really a problem about omniscience. Omniscience should be thought of as *maximal degree of knowledge*... Historically, this perfection has often been understood in such a way that a being x is omniscient only if for every proposition p, x knows whether p is true.... This of course involves quantification over all propositions. Now you suggest there is a problem here: we *can't* quantify over all propositions, because Cantorian arguments show that there aren't any... propositions about all propositions... But suppose you're right: what we have, then, is not a difficulty for *omniscience* as such, but for one way of explicating omniscience, one way of saying what this maximal perfection with respect to knowledge is.[7]

Unlike van Inwagen, Plantinga is not explicitly relying on the claim that God is the greatest possible being. But that claim seems to be just behind the scenes. For Plantinga's claim is that we can safely deny that God is classically omniscient if this denial is consistent with the claim that God has the maximal—i.e., the greatest possible—degree of knowledge. And this is presumably 'permissible tinkering' with the concept of God because it does not contravene the principle that God is the greatest possible being. After all, if classical omniscience is impossible, there is no fear that some other possible being might, by possessing classical omniscience, be greater than God.

Standard responses to paradoxes of omnipotence proceed in a similar vein. Abstracting from details, a standard line of reply to paradoxes of this sort hold that they illicitly suppose that God's omnipotence requires God to have an impossible property—like the property of creating a stone that God could not lift. But, so the standard reply goes, this is an impossible property, and hence one which we can deny

---

[7] Plantinga and Grim (1993), 291.

to God without contradicting the principle that God is the greatest possible being. It is, therefore, dispensable.[8]

This is enough, I hope, to show that the perfect being defense is very widely deployed. Recently, this defense has been significantly generalized in the work of Yujin Nagasawa. In his 'A New Defence of Anselmian Theism,' Nagasawa distinguishes between the Anselmian Thesis—roughly, the claim that God is the greatest possible being[9]— and the OmniGod Thesis—the claim that God is omnipotent, omniscient, and omnibenevolent. Nagasawa then points out that arguments against the existence of God typically target the claim that God has one or more of the omni-properties rather than the Anselmian Thesis itself. The theist who endorses [Conditions] thus has room to resist these arguments by denying the conditional claim that if the Anselmian Thesis is true, then the OmniGod Thesis is true. This point he, says, 'undercuts existing arguments against Anselmian theism *all at once.*'[10]

The reason why it undercuts these arguments 'all at once' is that such arguments all try to show either that one of the divine attributes is individually impossible, or that two or more are jointly incompossible. But such arguments inevitably rely on assumptions about just what the attributes of God are supposed to be. Such assumptions are licensed by the OmniGod Thesis—but they are not licensed by the claim that God

---

[8] Parallel points could be made about replies to arguments for the incompatibility of omnipotence with essential goodness of the sort given in Pike (1969). Standard replies rely on the claim that these arguments assume that God is omnipotent in a sense which is inconsistent with essential perfect goodness, and hence that the conjunctive property—being omnipotent in the sense presupposed by these arguments and being essentially perfectly good—is impossible, and hence dispensable. Often, of course, this line of defense is buttressed with an alternative account of omnipotence.

[9] I say 'roughly' because Nagasawa formulates it as the claim that God is the being than which no greater can be thought, rather than in explicitly modal terms. But since his argument (as far as I can see) does not rely on a distinction between what can be thought and what is possible, I stick with the modal formulation for simplicity. Nagasawa's preferred way of making the Anselmian Thesis more explicit—the MaximalGod Thesis—is given in explicitly modal terms. See Nagasawa (2008), 586. More on the distinction between conceivability and possibility in this context in §6.4 below.

[10] Nagasawa (2008), 578. Emphasis in original.

is the greatest possible being since, as Nagasawa points out, it seems to be epistemically possible that God is the greatest possible being but not the bearer of all of the omni-properties.

Nagasawa's defense of Anselmian Theism is an instance of what I have been calling the perfect being defense. To see this, note that his preferred replacement for the OmniGod Thesis is

'*The MaximalGod Thesis.*  God is the being that has the maximal consistent set of knowledge, power and benevolence.'[11]

which is equivalent to the conjunction of the claim that God is the greatest possible being with the auxiliary assumption that a being's greatness supervenes on its knowledge, power, and benevolence. But if the MaximalGod Thesis captures our concept of God, we can see immediately that if, for example, classical omniscience is impossible, then this property is not one which our concept of God requires God to have. That concept, after all, requires only that God have the maximal *consistent* combination of knowledge, power, and benevolence. Hence classical omniscience is, if impossible, dispensable.

Indeed, the claim that any such impossible property is, in virtue of being impossible, dispensable, is required for Nagasawa's defense to have the generality he claims for it. His defense is, he says, 'a radically new and more economical response to Anselmian theism, one that aims to eliminate the force of the arguments against it *all at once*.'[12] But since he does not engage with the details of any argument against Anselmian Theism—indeed, the point of his more economical new defense is to obviate the need for that—Nagasawa's defense eliminates the force of an argument against Anselmian Theism just in case it enables us to treat the property targeted by any anti-Anselmian argument as dispensable. Viewed in this light, Nagasawa's 'New Defence' is simply the consistent and universal employment of the principles— [Dispensable] and its apparent corollary [Impossible]—characteristic of the perfect being defense.

[11] Nagasawa (2008), 586.     [12] Nagasawa (2008), 585. Emphasis in original.

## 6.2 A reductio of the perfect being defense

Something should strike us as odd about the dialectical situation here. On the one hand, non-theists attempt to provide arguments against the existence of God by showing that one or more candidates for divine attributes are individually or jointly impossible. On the other hand, proponents of the perfect being defense are licensed, for any property demonstrated to be impossible, to dismiss that property as dispensable. The non-theist would thus appear to be in a rather unenviable position; the very success of her arguments is simply grist for the mill of the perfect being defense.

One might regard this as a great victory for the theist. Alternatively, one might think that this shows that there is something fishy about the perfect being defense. I now want to argue that the latter view is the correct one. (I'll turn in the next section to the question of *why* the perfect being defense goes wrong.)

Suppose that the non-theist presents an argument for the inconsistency of the following three theses:

(a) God is omnipotent.
(b) God is perfectly good.
(c) God created a universe which contains some evil.

Arguments of this general form are of course very familiar, as are many standard responses. Often arguments of this sort rely on eminently questionable assumptions, like the assumption that a perfectly good being will always eliminate as much evil as it can, or the assumption that an omnipotent being can create any possible world; and theists typically respond to arguments of this form by identifying, and rejecting, the relevant assumptions.

But the perfect being defense would seem to license a much simpler and more general response to this form of argument. She can simply pose the following dilemma to the non-theist: either the conjunctive property

omnipotent & perfectly good & creator of a universe with evil in it is possible, or it is not. If it is possible, then the non-theist's attempt to demonstrate the inconsistency of (a)–(c) fails. If it is impossible, then it is not a property of the greatest possible being, and hence is dispensable. Either way, the non-theist's argument fails. Q.E.D.

The non-theist, undaunted, might try again. She might come up with a yet more clever argument for the inconsistency of the following theses:

(d) God is very powerful.
(e) God is very good.
(f) God created a universe with amount $E$ of evil.

where it is plausible that the universe in fact contains amount $E$ of evil. But, no matter how clever the argument, the perfect being defender is ready with a response. Either the properties attributed to God by (d)–(f) are jointly possible, or they are not. If they are, then the argument for the inconsistency of (d)–(f) fails. (Who cares where?) If they are not, then the conjunctive property corresponding to (d)–(f) is impossible, and hence dispensable. So again the argument fails.

Nor is there anything special here about arguments from evil. We can consider any one of the examples used in Chapter 2 to illustrate the range of GIP-properties to make the same point. Recall, for example, Singularity:

The universe, of necessity, begins with expansion from a high density singularity. Necessarily, everything that exists is causally 'downstream' from this singularity. In different worlds, the universe unfolds differently—partly due to variation in the laws of nature, and partly due to chance. But the laws can only vary in a tight band, and it is impossible for the laws to be such as to permit the evolution of organisms significantly more intelligent or powerful than human beings.

Let us say that, if Singularity is true, that the greatest possible amount of power, goodness, and knowledge is $X$. Surely, given the above description, we can see that nothing with property $X$ would be God; after all, a being with property $X$ would not have more power, knowledge, or goodness than a human being. Given this, if the above description of the universe is correct, then God does not exist.

So surely, one thinks, a non-theist in possession of a convincing argument for Singularity has in her possession a good argument against the existence of God.

But, predictably, the perfect being defender has an answer. For if the above hypothesis is correct, then nothing could be greater than something with property $X$. So every other property which would be greater to have than $X$ is not possibly instantiated and hence, by [Impossible], a dispensable property.[13]

To put the same point in Nagasawa's terms, there is nothing in Singularity which implies the falsity of the MaximalGod Thesis. (After all, the non-theist has no argument for the claim that nothing with property $X$ actually exists.) So if the MaximalGod thesis does indeed capture the commitments of the Anselmian theist, the latter should find an argument for the above view of the universe profoundly untroubling.

It is clear at this point, I take it, that something has gone badly wrong; the truth of Singularity obviously entails the truth of atheism. So things simply can't be this easy for the theist. But, if you agree with this verdict, you must also agree that there is something wrong with the perfect being defense. For if the perfect being defense were legitimate, there would be nothing wrong with the theist's imagined responses to different versions of the argument from evil, or to an argument for Singularity. After all, if the perfect being defense is in general legitimate, then it really is true that any impossible property, just in virtue of being impossible, is dispensable.[14]

---

[13] See Oppy (2011) for an excellent discussion of similar scenarios in which the greatest possible being would fall short of being God.

[14] While this argument opposes Nagasawa's 'New Defence' (as it opposes any instance of the perfect being defense) it is worth highlighting the fact that I am agreeing with Nagasawa on one central point: it is epistemically possible (in at least one good sense of that term) that the Anselmian Thesis be true and the OmniGod Thesis false. What Nagasawa misses, I think, is that when one thinks of the range of cases which would falsify the second thesis but not the first, this turns out not to provide a general defense of Anselmian theism, but rather to falsify the characteristic Anselmian claim that our concept of God is the concept of a greatest possible being.

The parallels to the instances of the perfect being defense discussed in the previous section are fairly clear. The dilemma which we just imagined the theist posing to the proponent of various versions of the argument from evil is exactly parallel to the dilemma which van Inwagen poses for the atheist attempting to demonstrate the incompatibility of free will and omniscience. And all of the instances of the perfect being defense we discussed rely on the validity of the inference from impossibility to dispensability—which is the only premise required for the envisaged response to the argument from evil, or Singularity, to stick.

Let me emphasize that I am not saying that van Inwagen's response to the incompatibility of free will and foreknowledge, or any of the other instances of the perfect being defense mentioned above, is as implausible as the envisaged response to the problem of evil. On the contrary, classical omniscience does strike me as a much more plausible candidate for a dispensable attribute than the conjunctive properties attributed by (a)–(c) or (d)–(f) above, or the property of being greater than something with property $X$. What I am saying is that the perfect being defense itself provides no help in making this distinction; it validates the bad response to the problem of evil just as readily as the others.

## 6.3 The perfect being defense: a diagnosis

The argument of the preceding section shows that the use of [Dispensable] and its apparent corollary [Impossible] by the perfect being defender to distinguish mandatory from dispensable attributes should be rejected. But it does not tell us why this apparently promising strategy goes wrong.

The perfect being defender can be thought of as pursuing the following chain of reasoning:

(i) The claim that God is the greatest possible being captures the core of our conception of God;

(ii) So, if denying that God is $F$ does not contradict the claim that God is the greatest possible being, then denying that God is $F$ does not contradict the core of our conception of God;

(iii) So, if denying that God is $F$ does not contradict the claim that God is the greatest possible being, $F$ is dispensable;

(iv) If a property $F$ is impossible, then denying that God is $F$ won't contradict the claim that God is the greatest possible being, since in that case there will be no possible $F$ which could exceed God's greatness;

(v) So, from (iii) and (iv), it follows that any impossible property is dispensable.

This reasoning fails in two places. The most important of these is (i).

What the reductio arguments of the preceding section demonstrate is that the claim that God is the greatest possible being does not capture the core of our conception of God. At best, it can capture the core of our conception of God only if it is combined with certain theses about modal space.

The problem is one that we have already noticed: certain theories about the nature of the universe will, so to speak, 'shrink' modal space. Singularity is one example; but there are, as the discussion of GIP-properties in §2.4 showed, plenty of others. Many such hypotheses will entail that it is impossible that there be anything great enough for us to be remotely inclined to regard that being as God. But, despite this, many will be consistent with the existence of a greatest possible being. Singularity, for instance, while clearly inconsistent with the existence of God, is not clearly inconsistent with the existence of a greatest possible being, or a being which has the greatest possible combination of power, knowledge, and goodness.

The theist, it may be worth adding, is in no position to object that there is something illegitimate abut this sort of shrinking of modal space, for the 'possibility' that modal space may be in certain respects smaller than we think is a tool frequently deployed by theists. To take one well-known example: it has been argued (in a number of related ways) that God's omnipotence is inconsistent with God's being essentially perfectly good. For if God is omnipotent, then God can bring about any possible state of affairs; so, it is possible that God bring about some morally prohibited state of affairs; so, God is possibly less than perfectly good, and therefore not essentially perfectly good.[15]

The standard theistic reply to this sort of argument is nicely articulated by Thomas Morris. Given God's necessary goodness, Morris says,

No state of affairs whose actualization . . . would be such that God would be blameworthy in intentionally bringing it about or allowing it . . . represents a genuine possibility. Thus, on any careful definition of omnipotence, God's inability to actualize such a state of affairs no more detracts from his omnipotence than does his inability to create spherical cubes . . . [here] we find an important corollary of the Anselmian conception of God brought to light. Such a God is a delimiter of possibilities. If there is a being who exists necessarily, and is necessarily omnipotent, omniscient, and good, then many states of affairs which would otherwise represent genuine possibilities, and which by all non-theistic tests of logic and semantics do represent possibilities, are strictly impossible in the strongest sense.[16]

The present point is that it is not only the hypothesis that God is a necessarily omniscient, omnipotent, and perfectly good being which is a delimiter of possibilities; various anti-theistic hypotheses similarly delimit modal space. And the claim that God is the greatest possible being can only hope to capture the core of our conception of God when it is conjoined with the highly substantive claim that none of these anti-theist modal-space-delimiting hypotheses are true.

Here is a more informal way to see what is wrong with step (i) of the perfect being defender's reasoning. Suppose that one were to hold that the claim that God is the greatest actual being captures the core of our conception of God. One way to show that this is a mistake is to imagine that, at the end of the universe, it turns out that Michael Jordan was the most impressive being to ever have existed. Then atheism is true, because, as it turns out, this universe did not turn out to include any being great enough to be God. Being the best would not make Jordan

---

[15] See, among other places, Pike (1969); Resnick (1973); Guleserian (1983).
[16] Morris (1985), 47–8.

God; so the claim that God is the greatest actual being does not capture the core of our conception of God.

But just as whether the best thing in the universe is God depends on what the universe contains, so the question of whether the best thing in the pluriverse—the space of all possible worlds—is God depends on what the pluriverse contains. It depends on what is and is not possible.

One somewhat fanciful way to press the point is to imagine a philosopher coming up with a surprising argument, based on some strong actualist premises, for the conclusion that it is impossible that anything be greater than the greatest actual thing. This argument, plus the claim that something in the actual world is such that nothing is actually better than it, should not convince anyone that God exists. It should just convince them (if they don't think that God actually exists) that the pluriverse is depressingly bereft of truly excellent things.

This has all been by way of criticizing step (i) of the perfect being defender's line of reasoning above. But there is another (much less important) problem, which emerges at step (iv). This step lays out the reasoning which led us from [Dispensable] to [Impossible]. The basic idea is that if some property $F$ is impossible, then denying that God is $F$ cannot imply that God is less than the greatest possible being, since one is then simply denying God a property which no possible being has.

What this plausible-sounding argument misses is that it may be the case that some properties are such that their impossibility implies that it is impossible that there be a greatest possible being. That is, it may be that the impossibility of some property $F$ implies that for any object $x$ in any world $w$, there is some object $y$ and world $w^*$ such that $y_{w^*} > x_w$. Suppose, just to pick one example, that we identify the maximum conceivable levels of power, knowledge, and goodness; call these perfections $P$, $K$, and $G$. Now suppose that we find that none of $P$, $K$, and $G$ are possibly instantiated. If none of these are possibly instantiated, it might follow that for every possible being, there is another possible being more powerful than it, some other possible being more knowledgeable than it, and some other possible being better than it. And in that case it will plausibly follow from the fact that none of P, K, and G are possibly instantiated that it is impossible that there be a greatest possible being.

This will then falsify the right-hand side of [Conditions] and hence—by the lights of the theist who holds that his principle states the conditions under which God exists—entail the non-existence of God. It is, therefore, not dispensable. What this shows is that even if [Dispensable] were correct—and the argument of the first half of this section shows that it is not—[Impossibility] would still not follow. This is because denying that some impossible properties hold of God implies that there is no greatest possible being, not by making room for some other possible being with the relevant attribute, but rather by making the property of being the greatest possible being itself impossible.

## 6.4 The epistemic perfect being defense

Let's now consider a modification of the perfect being defense—one which is naturally suggested by the problems which arose from 'possibility-shrinking' non-theistic hypotheses in the preceding section. This is the idea that when formulating our distinction between dispensable and mandatory attributes, we should focus, not on the claim that God is the greatest possible being, but on the claim that God is the greatest conceivable being.

One of the central worries of the previous two sections was that it might turn out that certain properties are, even though not possibly instantiated, nonetheless mandatory rather than dispensable. In the case of Singularity, one prominent such property was the property of having more power, knowledge, and goodness than a being with property X—where such a being would not have significantly more power, knowledge, or goodness than a normal human being. But even if Singularity implies that having this property is not possible, it does not imply that having this property is not conceivable. Quite the contrary; no matter what the contours of (alethic) modal space turn out to be, we can surely imagine, or conceive of, a being with much greater power, knowledge, and goodness than any human being. The shift from possibility to conceivability thus promises to solve the problem illustrated by the too-easy responses to the argument from evil and examples like Singularity discussed above, much as the shift from alethic to epistemic perfect being theology promised to solve the problem posed by the diversity of GIP-properties.

It is natural, then, to think that we might formulate the perfect being defense in epistemic rather than alethic terms. And, by adapting the framework developed above, there is a natural way to do this. One who claims that the core of our concept of God is given by the claim that God is the greatest conceivable being will state the conditions under which God exists not with [Conditions], but with a principle like the following:

[Conditions*]   God exists iff $\exists x$ (we cannot conceive of a being greater than $x$ is in $\alpha$)[17]

This says that God exists just in case there is something which is such that we can imagine nothing greater.

As above, we can use this principle to state a sufficient condition for a property to be dispensable:

[Dispensable*]   If the proposition that God is not $F$ does not entail the falsity of the right-hand side of [Conditions*], then $F$ is dispensable.

And, if [Conditions*] does capture the core of our conception of God, this principle is a very reasonable one. For suppose that denying that God (or anything else) is $F$ does not imply that there is no being than which none greater can be thought. Then this denial is consistent with the claim that there exists a being which satisfies the core of our

---

[17] We could state this in a way more closely parallel to [GPB] by quantifying over conceivable beings and conceivable worlds; the formulation above will be enough for present purposes.

conception of God—and hence the property we are denying God to have must be a dispensable one.

As discussed in Chapter 3, it is notorious that there are many different senses of 'conceivable.' The proponent of the epistemic perfect being defense thus owes an answer to the question of which of these gives the intended interpretation of [Conditions*].

Fortunately for the reader, it is not necessary to consider each definition in the laundry list canvassed in Chapter 3. The same dilemma on which epistemic perfect being theology founders also shows that the epistemic perfect being defense is a failure.

I argued in Chapter 3 that every definition of conceivability falls into one of two categories. On the one hand, the definition might collapse conceivability into possibility—so that claims about God are conceivable (in the relevant sense) iff they are necessary. On the other hand, the definition might entail the existence of trouble-makers— properties such that (i) it is conceivable (in the relevant sense) that God has them, (ii) it is impossible that God has them, and (iii) it is better for God to have them than lack them.

Definitions of conceivability in the first category collapse the epistemic perfect being defense into the alethic perfect being defense, and so are of no use to us here.

Definitions of conceivability in the second category are also useless to the epistemic perfect being theologian. This is because they will make it too easy to show that God does not exist. A trouble-maker is a property which God lacks and which is such that something with the property would be (per impossibile) greater than anything with it. From the existence of such a property it follows that the right-hand side of [Conditions*] is false, which (given the truth of that biconditional) entails that God does not exist. This is of course an immediate result of the problem for epistemic perfect being theology discussed in Chapter 3, which was that definitions of 'conceivable' which entail the existence of trouble-makers falsify the principle that God is the greatest conceivable (in that sense) being.

So the proponent of the epistemic perfect being defense needs a definition of 'conceivable' which falls into neither of these two categories; it neither collapses the conceivable into the possible, nor permits the existence of trouble-makers. As in Chapter 3, I have no impossibility proof to offer. But I think that the catalogue of candidates examined there should make us very pessimistic that there is a stable middle ground to be found.

# 7

# Perfect Being Semantics

So far we've looked at two questions which the modal conception of God seemed well-suited to answer:

- What are the divine attributes?
- What properties are non-negotiable, core parts of our concept of God?

We've seen that, in the end, it does not help us find the answer to either. In this chapter I want to look at one last theoretical role which the principle that God is the greatest possible being has been enlisted to play: the role of, in some way or other, explaining the meaning of the name 'God.' Let's call the view that the description 'the greatest possible being' can play some role of this sort *perfect being semantics.*[1]

As we'll see below, many advocates of perfect being theology say things which make it clear that they would endorse some form or another of perfect being semantics. But it is also true that many advocates of perfect being theology who do not make explicit claims about the relationship between the meaning of 'God' and the description 'the greatest possible being' still claim that this description, in some sense, captures our *concept* of God. And this is but a short remove from perfect being semantics, since, if there is such a thing as our concept of God, that concept would seem to be a natural candidate to play a role in explaining the meaning of 'God.'

---

[1] I intend this label to be broad enough to include theorists who would use instead the description 'the greatest conceivable being' or 'the greatest actual being.' I discuss these alternatives below.

# 7.1 The standard picture of names

Following the work of Saul Kripke, many philosophers and linguists take the following to be true of many ordinary proper names:[2]

- Names acquire a reference at the time in which they are introduced. Names are introduced (as it is often said) by a kind of *dubbing*: they are introduced as a tag for an object which the person or persons introducing the name can already, through independent means, call to mind. This may or may not involve perceptual acquaintance with the object; but the object named is one to which the introducers are already able to make singular reference, rather than one which can only be designated as the thing, whatever it is, which satisfies a certain description. Let's, for lack of a better term, call names which meet this condition *dubbing-introduced*.

- Later users of the name are, in a certain way, parasitic on the way in which the name is introduced. These later users need not associate the name with any description which uniquely singles out its referent, nor must they know anything about the context in which the name was introduced. Rather, their intentions to use the name with the same reference as those from whom they acquired it, and their connection via other language users to the introduction of the name, are sufficient for the name, as they use it, to refer to the object which the name was introduced to refer to. Let's call names which meet this condition *Kripkean* names.

- The semantic content of a name is not given by any description which speakers may or may not associate with the name. Instead, the semantic content of a name just is the object to which the name refers. Names which meet this condition are *Millian* names.

---

[2] See especially Kripke (1972). Kripke argued that most names have the first two of the three characteristics listed. He does not argue directly for Millianism, though arguments he gave against certain non-Millian views are widely taken to be the central arguments in favor of a Millian view. See, for example, Soames (2002).

This is oversimplified in certain respects;[3] but these conditions provide, as Kripke put it, a kind of 'picture' of the functioning of names which seems to fit many ordinary proper names quite well. I'll say that names which satisfy all three of these conditions are *ordinary names*.

## 7.2 Three grades of perfect being semantics

If 'God' were an ordinary name, then the description 'the greatest possible being' would play no role in explaining how the name was introduced, in explaining the competence conditions for users of the name, or in giving the semantic content of the name. So the perfect being semanticist must deny that 'God' is an ordinary name. And, while 'God' does look at first glance like a run of the mill proper name, it is plausible enough that not all expressions which look superficially like names are really ordinary names.

Let's look at three sorts of examples of expressions which superficially appear to be names but are not, in the above sense, ordinary names.

The first are cases of explicit abbreviation. Suppose that we find ourselves using some description very frequently—say 'the tallest squirrel in the yard right now.' We might become tired of using this phrase, and decide to introduce an abbreviation—say, 'Goliath'—for the description.

This will in some ways appear to be a name; we can utter a sentence like 'Goliath is eating out of the birdfeeder right now' which, at least superficially, looks like a sentence in which a name is combined with a complex one-place predicate. But, given that all users of the name

---

[3] To mention just two: (i) no one thinks that 'intending to use the name in the same way as earlier users' is quite sufficient for the name to maintain its reference over time, as well-known examples of reference shift like 'Madagascar' show. (The example is due to Evans (1973). For recent discussion, see Burgess (2014).) (ii) Many take the semantic content of a name to be nondescriptional, but deny that names are Millian, because they take the semantic contents of names to be nondescriptive Fregean modes of presentation. (See, for example, McDowell (1977).) These sorts of complications won't matter for what follows.

intend to use it as an abbreviation of 'the tallest squirrel in the yard right now,' it is hard to believe that it could differ in its meaning from that description. It will, for instance, single out different squirrels with respect to different contexts of use, and hence will be, like the description it abbreviates, an indexical. We might ask, for instance, 'Who is Goliath right now? Is it that one?'

To claim that 'Goliath' has the same meaning as the description with which it is associated is just to say that abbreviation is not semantically significant. As Gareth Evans says, 'We do not produce new thoughts . . . simply by a "stroke of pen" . . . simply by introducing a name into the language.'[4] Since 'Goliath' has the same content as the associated description, it is not a Millian name. Instead, I'll say, it is *semantically descriptive*. One view that the perfect being semanticist might take is that 'God' is semantically descriptive, and has the same semantic content as 'the greatest possible being.'

Let's look at a second sort of example of an expression which appears to be a name, but is not in fact an ordinary name. Suppose that every morning after a rain my daughter finds some small animal footprints in the mud outside our house. She can't tell what sort of animal it is, but the footprints always look quite similar. She might then introduce the name 'Morton' for the animal, whatever it is, that makes the footprints every night. The other members of the family might then pick up this usage from her. We can suppose that the description 'the animal that makes the footprints in the mud every night' becomes conventionally associated with 'Morton' in a certain way: every person who counts as a competent user of 'Morton' must associate the description with the name, and take the name to refer to the thing (if such there is) that uniquely satisfies the description.

'Morton' is not a Kripkean name, since every competent user of the name is required to associate the name with the description 'the animal that makes the footprints in the mud every night,' and is disposed to take the name to refer to the unique satisfier of the description. I'll say that names of this sort are *description-associated*. But we have

---

[4] Evans (1982), 50.

made no explicit claims about the meaning of the name. For all we have said, 'Morton' could be a Millian name for the relevant animal. There seems to be room, then, for the perfect being semanticist to hold that 'God' is description-associated even if it is not semantically descriptive.

Now, perhaps the apparent space between examples like 'Goliath' and examples like 'Morton' is an illusion, and any name which is description-associated would just abbreviate the description and hence would not be a Millian name. Perhaps it is impossible for content and competence conditions to come apart in the way that they would have to for Millian but description-associated names to exist. But Kripke, for one, seems to leave open the possibility of names that are description-associated but not semantically descriptive.[5] In what follows I will assume that names can be description-associated without being semantically descriptive, in order to give the perfect being semanticist maximum room to maneuver. If it turns out that this is not possible, then that is just one less option for the perfect being semanticist.

Let's turn to a third way in which a description might play an important role in explaining the functioning of a name, which provides a final avenue for the perfect being semanticist. One might hold that the description 'the greatest possible being' is involved in determining the reference of 'God,' but does not do so in such a way that every competent user of 'God' must associate the description with the name, or be disposed to fix its reference by looking for the thing which satisfies the description.

There are well-known examples which might provide a model here. One is the example of 'Neptune', which (we can suppose) Leverrier

---

[5] Kripke obviously took this to be a live possibility in *Naming and Necessity*, since he did not take the modal argument against the view that names are semantically equivalent to descriptions to discredit the view that names have their reference fixed by description, and assumed that names whose reference was fixed by description were (in the present sense) description-associated.

introduced as a name for the thing, if such there is, which satisfies the description

the planet causing irregularities in the orbit of Uranus.

It appears that 'Neptune,' for Leverrier, functions much as 'Morton' functioned in the example given above.

But now consider Leverrier's colleague Arago. Leverrier may have confided to Arago that he was searching for a planet called 'Neptune,' but declined, perhaps out of fear that someone would discover the planet before him, to share the reference-fixing description. Arago might go on to use the name to refer to the planet; he might, for instance, say to someone else

If Leverrier is right, Neptune is a planet.

And Arago might do so despite the fact that he does not associate the above description with the name. But, despite the fact that he does not associate the description with the name, there is still a clear sense in which the name, out of his mouth, does owe its reference to a certain description: the reference of 'Neptune' out of Arago's mouth is parasitic on its reference out of Leverrier's mouth, and Leverrier explicitly associates the name with the relevant description.

Names like 'Neptune' need not be semantically descriptive, and need not be description-associated (since one can be a competent user of the name without being aware that it was ever associated with the relevant description). So 'Neptune' might well be a Millian and Kripkean name. But names like this are not dubbing-introduced. I'll say that names of this sort are, by contrast, *descriptively introduced*. A third view that the perfect being semanticist might take, then, is that 'God' is, like Neptune, descriptively introduced, with the relevant description being 'the greatest possible being.'

A quick terminological note: in setting up these three roles that a description might play in explaining the functioning of a name, I have conspicuously avoided employing the category of names whose 'reference is fixed by description.' The reason is that this phrase is sometimes used to pick out names which are (in the terminology just introduced) description-associated, and other times used to pick out names which are merely description-introduced. Kripke used the expression in the former way; he assumed that if a name had its reference fixed by description, then competent speakers would know that the referent of the name would have to satisfy the description.[6] In later discussions, though, 'fixed by description' is sometimes used to mean just 'introduced via description.'[7] So, even at the cost of introducing new terminology, it seems best to simply avoid the disputed phrase.

This gives us three exclusive, even if perhaps not exhaustive, distinctions:

Millian vs. semantically descriptive
Kripkean vs. description-associated
dubbing-introduced vs. descriptively introduced

And this gives us three theses which the perfect being semanticist might endorse: she might hold that 'God' is semantically descriptive, that it is description-associated, or that it is descriptively introduced.

It is worth keeping these theses separate. Sometimes the thesis that 'God' is directly referential—i.e. Millian—is presented as opposed to the thesis that the reference of 'God' is determined by a description associated with the name by speakers.[8] But this is a false opposition if a name can be (as Kripke assumed) Millian but description-associated.

This is one dimension, then, along which different versions of perfect being semantics might differ. But they might also differ in their choice of the modal principle they take to provide the relevant description. Is the functioning of 'God' to be explained in terms of 'the greatest conceivable being,' 'the greatest possible being,' or 'the greatest actual being'?

Fortunately for our purposes, the differences between the first two won't matter for the argument of this chapter. The reason is the

---

[6] Were this not so, the epistemic argument against the view that names have their reference fixed by description would make no sense. See Lecture II of Kripke (1972).

[7] See, for example, Berger (2002).

[8] As in Alston (1988).

dilemma presented in Chapter 3, and discussed again in §6.4. It is very hard to find a definition of 'conceivable' which both avoids collapsing conceivability into possibility and does not falsify the principle that God is the greatest conceivable (in the relevant sense) being. Definitions in the former category will be no real alternative to alethic formulations, and definitions in the latter category will trivially entail (given the truth of some version of epistemic perfect being semantics) that 'God' fails to refer. So, in what follows I set aside formulations of perfect being semantics in epistemic terms, and focus on alethic perfect being semantics.

Occasionally, the difference between 'greatest possible' and 'greatest actual' formulations will be relevant; when this is the case, I make note of it. Otherwise I'll focus on the description 'the greatest possible being' for simplicity.

## 7.3 What is special about 'God'?

Advocates of perfect being theology often endorse, or say things which seem to immediately entail, all three of our 'perfect being semantics' theses. Katherin Rogers, for instance, writes that

> ... I am using 'God' as a descriptive name, a title such that anything than which a greater *can* be thought is just not God. ... if we are so 'weak and foolish' as to use the term 'God' of a being whom we judge to be imperfect and than whom we can conceive of a better, I would say we are not really thinking of God at all.[9]

In a similar vein, Mark Johnston writes

> In fact, it is quite unclear whether 'God,' as we now use it, is a *name* at all, as opposed to a compressed title, in effect something like 'the Supreme Being' or 'the Most High.' ...

> If 'God' as we now use it is a name in any sense, it clearly does not function like an ordinary proper name. In its function, it is closest to what philosophers

[9] Rogers (2000), 4–5. In using 'weak and foolish' Rogers is quoting a passage from Alston (1988).

call a *descriptive name*, a name that in some way abbreviates a description and so is tied to that description for its meaning.[10]

Sometimes, the discussion is couched in terms of the concept of God rather than the meaning of the name 'God', as in this striking passage from Peter van Inwagen:

> I should also be willing to count the following position as a form (a very unusual one, to be sure) of atheism: Some (existent) person enjoys—essentially—the highest degree of greatness that is metaphysically possible, and, in some other possible world, some other being enjoys that degree of greatness. (It is therefore conceptually possible—the concept 'atheist' does not rule out this bizarre possibility—that there should be an atheist who believes that the universe was created *ex nihilo* by an omniscient, omnipotent, perfectly good being who is the unique exemplar of these excellent features in every possible world in which it exists.) In sum: the concept of God is the concept of a person whose degree of greatness cannot be excelled or equaled by any other possible being.[11]

But while phrased in terms of the concept of God, it is hard to separate these claims from claims about the meaning of 'God.' For if there is such a thing as the concept of God, it is the concept expressed by 'God.' And presumably the concept expressed by 'God' just is the meaning of 'God.' So if the concept of God is identical to the concept of a greatest possible being, it is hard to avoid the conclusion that 'God' is semantically equivalent to the description 'the greatest possible being.'

Indeed, given this apparent link between the concept of God and the meaning of 'God', it would seem that one form or another of perfect being semantics is a very widely held view. For, at least among perfect being theologians, the claim that a principle like [GPB] is not just true of, but also captures the concept of, God is very widely endorsed.

Perfect being semanticists typically do not rely on an opposition to the general thesis that at least many names are Kripkean, Millian,

---

[10] Johnston (2011), 6–8. To be sure, Johnston would probably not self-identify as a 'perfect being theologian.' But his theological program has much in common with perfect being theology. For an excellent discussion, see Chignell and Zimmerman (2012).

[11] van Inwagen (2006), Ch. 2, note 10, 158.

and dubbing-introduced. Rather, they think that, even if most names are ordinary names, 'God' is not. Why do they think this? There are, I think, three main arguments against the view that 'God' is an ordinary name.

### 7.3.1 The argument from the absence of dubbings

Considering the hypothesis that 'God' is an ordinary name, Mark Johnston objects that

> On this model, all the adherents of the different monotheisms would need to do is intend to connect with a chain of reference that leads back to some primordial dubbing of some being with some original, say Hebrew, form of the name 'God.' . . .

> However, that is not how 'God' works. In the scriptures, no one actually turns up and says anything like 'I am to be called by *the name* "God."' No one says anything like 'I hereby introduce *the name* "God" as the name of THIS very impressive being.' There is no original dubbing of someone or something as 'God,' a dubbing that we now can hope to fall back on.[12]

If this is right, then 'God' is not dubbing-introduced, and so is not an ordinary name.

### 7.3.2 The argument from requirements on reference

One version of the second sort of argument is presented by Jordan Howard Sobel in the following passage:

> 'God' is not like most names, if, as I think, that it would name in common use One who would be the true god is settled by linguistic convention and is not defeasible. Suppose believers became convinced that what they had been meaning to refer to with the name 'God'—the god of Abraham, Isaac, and Jacob—was in fact no god at all, but an ancient all-too-human practical joker named David who burnt bushes and the rest. These believers would not say, 'That joker David, what a come-down for God.' They would say that they had been mistaken in thinking that they, and those before them, Abraham, Isaac, and Jacob, had been referring to God . . . , for David was no god, and That One would need to have been one.[13]

---

[12] Johnston (2011), 5–6. Emphasis in the original.
[13] Sobel (2004), 5. For a similar argument involving 'Jesus' rather than 'God,' see Harris (1991), 81–2.

The argument can be put as a reductio of the thesis that 'God' is an ordinary name. If 'God' were an ordinary name, then there would have to be an introduction of that name which fixed its reference. Suppose that this is the occasion of Moses' encounter with the burning bush. Then 'God' would refer to whatever was the source of the voice Moses heard. But it is coherent to suppose that this was in fact the joker described. So, if 'God' were an ordinary name, it is coherent to suppose that 'God' refers to that joker. But that is not coherent. So 'God' is not an ordinary name.

More generally, the thought—which is also near the surface in the quote from van Inwagen—is that we can know in advance that nothing which lacked certain very special qualities could be the referent of 'God.' But if 'God' were an ordinary name, then it would be hard to see why this should be so. For then it would just refer to whatever the introducers of the name had in mind; and, as with other ordinary names, there is no reason to think that any facts about the way in which the name was introduced would be evident to us later users of the name.

If, on the other hand, 'God' is either semantically descriptive, description-associated, or descriptively introduced, it will follow from these facts about the name that nothing which did not satisfy the description could be its referent. And if, as the perfect being semanticist thinks, the relevant description is 'the greatest possible being,' this would plainly rule out the 'joker' scenario Sobel has in mind. So here perfect being semantics (of one form or another) seems to provide just what we want.

### 7.3.3 The argument from informative identities

The third argument is presented in the following passage from Mark Johnston:

Even if . . . Yahweh is in fact God, the name 'Yahweh' does not mean the same as 'God.' For it is coherent to doubt, as the second-century theologian Marcion did, whether Yahweh is in fact God. Marcion also doubted that the god who appeared to Abraham was God. If Marcion was wrong about this, then his mistakes were not about the meanings of words. They would be mistakes as to the theological facts of the matter. This itself entails that 'Yahweh' does not mean 'God,' and that 'God' does not mean 'the god who appeared to Abraham.' If those were equivalences in meaning, then there would be no room for the relevant factual mistakes.[14]

Here I think that Johnston is supposing for the sake of argument that 'Yahweh' is an ordinary name. One can, as Marcion did, coherently doubt whether Yahweh is God. But if this is possible, then, the argument goes, 'God' must not be an ordinary name introduced in the way that 'Yahweh' was introduced, for then they would be guaranteed to have the same reference. But the argument appears to generalize for, given any ordinary name, it will always be coherent to wonder whether the bearer of that name is in fact God. So 'God' is not an ordinary name, in our sense.

This sort of argument can also be understood as establishing the stronger thesis that 'God' is semantically descriptive. For, Johnston suggests, the fact that we can coherently wonder whether the referent of 'God' is the referent of 'Yahweh' shows that the two are not semantically equivalent (do not mean the same thing). But presumably 'Yahweh' is a Millian name; so, if 'God' is a Millian name, it is not a Millian name for the thing which 'Yahweh' names. And again the argument would seem to generalize, since, for any Millian name, it would seem that one could coherently doubt whether the bearer of that name really is God. So 'God' must not be a Millian name.

If, by contrast, 'God' were semantically equivalent to 'the greatest possible being,' the phenomenon to which Johnston draws attention here would be easy to explain. For, given any ordinary name, it will always be possible to coherently wonder whether the bearer of that name is the greatest possible being. This is parallel to the fact that, if we introduced by dubbing a Kripkean/Millian name 'Francis' for some squirrel living in the yard, we could always intelligibly ask, 'Is Francis really Goliath?'

\* \* \*

These arguments describe phenomena which are prima facie hard to explain on the hypothesis that 'God' is an ordinary name, but easy

---

[14] Johnston (2011), 6.

to explain if some version of perfect being semantics is true. My aim in this chapter will be to examine our three versions of perfect being semantics on their own terms, to see if any provides a plausible account of the relevant aspect of 'God.' I'll argue that they do not. In Chapter 8, I'll return to the question of what the correct theory of the meaning of 'God' is, and how the opponent of perfect being semantics might reply to the arguments just sketched.

## 7.4 The modal conception and semantic equivalence

A natural suggestion for the proponent of the view that the modal conception of God gives 'our concept of God' is that 'God' is semantically equivalent to—has the same semantic content as—the description 'the greatest possible being.'

Natural as this idea is from a certain perspective, standard arguments against descriptivist theories of ordinary names show that it is difficult to sustain. If this view were true, then, given plausible compositionality assumptions, any pair of sentences which differ only in the substitution of 'God' for 'the greatest possible being' would—because they would differ only in the substitution of synonyms for synonyms—express the same proposition. Since sentences which express the same proposition cannot differ in truth-value, any such pair of sentences must—if the descriptivist account of the meaning of 'God' is true—have the same truth-value. The central problem is that it seems easy to find examples of pairs of sentences of this sort which differ in truth-value.

Which sentences these are depends on whether we are focusing on the description 'the greatest possible being' or 'the greatest actual being.' I'll begin by discussing three sorts of examples which are problematic for the view that 'God' is semantically equivalent to 'the greatest possible being': (i) examples involving theologically unsophisticated subjects; (ii) examples involving mildly heterodox subjects; and (iii) examples involving scenarios in which modal space

is, in a sense familiar from the examples in §2.4 and §6.2, impoverished. I'll then turn to the possibility that 'God' might be semantically
equivalent to 'the greatest actual being.'

### 7.4.1 Theologically unsophisticated subjects

The basic problem here was noticed by Aquinas, who pointed out that
'it is not known to all, even including those who admit that God exists,
that God is that than which a greater cannot be thought.'[15] To see
why this leads to a problem for the present version of perfect being
semantics, consider the sentence

My five-year-old daughter believes that God exists.

I think that this sentence is true. But, if the proposed descriptivist thesis were true, this sentence would be (given plausible compositionality
assumptions) synonymous with

My five-year-old daughter believes that the greatest possible being exists.

But this seems incorrect, since the second sentence seems false; despite
believing in God, I doubt whether my daughter has any explicitly
modal beliefs of this sort.

Some of the quotes sketched above suggest that some philosophers
will respond to this sort of example by simply denying that the first
sentence is true. On this view, my daughter doesn't really believe
in God, even if she utters sentences which, out of the mouth of a
competent user, obviously imply 'God exists.' Johnston, for instance,
says

Here is a fact about *descriptive* names: you can't use such a name with its
ordinary meaning without being disposed to use the description associated
with the name to determine the reference of the name.[16]

If 'God' is a descriptive name, and the relevant description is 'the
greatest possible being,' then, since children will not typically be
disposed to use a description like 'the greatest possible being' to fix
its reference, they are not (on this view) using 'God' with its ordinary

[15] *Summa Contra Gentiles* I.11.          [16] Johnston (2011), 8.

meaning.[17] So, whatever words may come out of their mouths, it is at best misleading to report their beliefs using 'God', as we ordinary users use the term.

So some perfect being semanticists may be inclined to bite the bullet on this one. But of course the problem is not just one about five-year-olds; many non-philosophically sophisticated speakers seem to use the term 'God' in normal ways without being disposed to fix its reference via any description of the imagined sort.[18] Imagine presenting an apparently ordinary adult user of the name 'God' with the following scenario:

> There is indeed an unimaginably great personal being which created the universe and everything in it, on which everything in the universe has always and always will depend, which has been in contact with human beings throughout history in such-and-such ways (fill in the content of one or another revealed religion here), which is perfectly good, and which offers salvation to all people. It is possible (for complicated theological reasons which needn't concern you) that there could have been an even greater being—but there isn't.

Without having done extensive surveys, I hypothesize that at least many ordinary users would say that, if that scenario is actual, then God exists. Whether or not they are correct about this, it is just not plausible that this should disqualify them from using 'God' with its

---

[17] To be sure, Johnston does not say unequivocally that the relevant description is 'the greatest possible being.' The closest he comes to identifying the relevant description is the following passage:

> Semanticists will ask: Do I mean 'the actual Highest One,' so that 'God' would denote the same being in any possible situation, even one in which a Higher One than any actual one exists? I do mean 'the actual Highest One,' but I also take it that if this description picks out anything, it picks out an entity that is such that there could not be a Higher in this world or in any other. There is a certain very High minimum that would have to be met by something if it is to be 'the Highest One.' I take it that this is part of the understanding of 'the Most High' and the like.
>
> (Johnston (2011), 12–13, note 4)

This suggests that he thinks that the description has some modal component, which is enough for present purposes.

[18] This point is emphasized in Alston (1988).

ordinary meaning, or should disqualify them from using the sentence 'God exists' to express their belief in God.

### 7.4.2 Heterodox subjects

Similar problems arise when we consider examples of theologically very sophisticated speakers who have either surprising views about modality, or mildly heterodox theological views.

For a case of the first sort, imagine that Jane is a theologically orthodox religious believer who also happens to be a skeptic about modal properties. It seems extremely plausible that

Jane believes that God exists.

will be true, but that

Jane believes that the greatest possible being exists.

will be false. But that is impossible if 'God' is semantically equivalent to 'the greatest possible being.'

We can also consider cases in which certain unusual combinations of theological views would make it plausible that a subject believes that God exists, but does not believe that the greatest possible being exists. In coming up with cases of the relevant sort, though, one must exercise some care. Rogers is right to ask,

. . . is it really a positive consequence [of the view that 'God' is an ordinary name] that worshippers of the petty, cruel, and adulterous Zeus are really worshipping the same being as those who worship Anselm's God and vice versa?[19]

It is, as Rogers says, not at all implausible to hold that belief in Zeus falls short of genuine belief in God. But this is because the characterization of Zeus that we get in classical Greek mythology differs so greatly from our conception of God.[20] Matters are much less clear if we imagine those whose theological views differ only very

---

[19] Rogers (2000), 5.
[20] See Chapter 8 below for some discussion of what I mean by 'our conception of God.'

slightly from ours, but who nonetheless deny that God is the greatest possible being.

To make a case concrete, let's look at a line of argument which might convince someone that God exists but that the greatest possible being does not. There are two parts to the argument. The first may be expressed by the following principle:

[Creation]   If $x$ in $w$ and $y$ in $w^*$ are alike except for the fact that $x$ in $w$ creates a better universe than does $y$ in $w^*$, then $x_w > y_{w^*}$

This principle seems, on its face, as plausible as other principles in the vicinity which are wielded by perfect being theologians. An omniscient being is thought to be better than a being which knows all but one proposition, on the grounds that knowledge is a good thing, and that knowing more is therefore greater than knowing less. Just so, creating a good universe is a good thing, and creating a better universe is greater than creating a worse one.

The second part of the argument comes from the claim that there are an infinite number of possible universes, some better than others, but none best of all. There are a number of routes to this conclusion; one emerges from Peter van Inwagen's discussion of the problem of evil.[21]

When van Inwagen turns to what he calls the 'local problem of evil,' he introduces the concept of a horror, and raises the question of why an omnipotent, omniscient, and perfectly good being would not prevent the existence of horrors. His answer comes in two parts. The first is that

... he has not done this because to have done it would have frustrated his plan for restoring human beings to their original union with him by removing an essential motive for cooperating with him—namely, the realization that there is something horribly wrong with the world they live in. The best that could come of a miraculous prevention of each of the horrors that resulted from our separation from God would be a state of perfect natural happiness ... But

---

[21] For a related view, see Schlesinger (1964).

allowing horrors to occur opens the possibility of a supernatural good for humanity that is infinitely better than perfect natural happiness.[22]

As van Inwagen quickly notes, this reply leads to a follow-up question: even if God had good reason to permit some horrors, why did God permit so many? Why did God not, instead, permit the minimum number of horrors required for God's plan? van Inwagen responds:

There is no minimum number of horrors consistent with God's plan of reconciliation, for the prevention of any one particular horror could not possibly have any effect on God's plan. For any $n$, if the existence of at most $n$ horrors is consistent with God's plan, the existence of at most $n - 1$ horrors will be equally consistent with God's plan.[23]

van Inwagen's thought here might be formulated like this:

For every universe consistent with God's plan, it is possible there is one with one less horror which is also consistent with God's plan.

But the following principle seems quite plausible:

If two possible universes $u$, $u^*$ differ only in that $u$ contains one less horror than $u^*$, then $u$ is a better universe than $u^*$

From these two claims together, it follows that

For every universe consistent with God's plan, it is possible that there is one better than it.

Presumably we are safe in assuming that no universe inconsistent with God's plan is better than any which is consistent with it. So we can conclude that

[No Best Universe]   For any universe, it is possible that there is one better than it.

And this is a thesis which, for reasons independent of the line of thought just sketched, has seemed appealing to many orthodox philosophers and theologians.[24]

---

[22] van Inwagen (2006), 104.   [23] van Inwagen (2006), 106.
[24] For a classical example, see *Summa Theologica* Ia.25.a6, reply 3.

Let's now help ourselves to the assumption, which most perfect being theologians will be happy to grant, that if there is a greatest possible being, that being creates a universe. Given this assumption, [Creation], and [No Best Universe], it is not hard to see how the argument for the conclusion that it is impossible that there be a greatest possible being can go:

Suppose for reductio that $G$ is the greatest possible being in some world $w$. We know that $G$ in $w$ creates a universe; call it $u$. By [No Best Universe], there could be a universe, $u^*$, better than $u$. There seems to be no reason why $u^*$ could not have been created by a being, $G^*$ (which may or may not be identical to $G$) which is like $G$ in every way but for the fact that $G$ creates $u$ and $G^*$ creates $u^*$. Let $w^*$ be a world in which $G^*$ creates $u^*$. Then it follows from [Creation] that $G^*_{w^*} > G_w$, which is contrary to our supposition.

Of course there are any number of steps in this chain of reasoning which can be resisted.[25] But my point is not that the argument I have just sketched is a good one. The point is just that one who finds this chain of reasoning plausible is not, just in virtue of finding it plausible, barred from using 'God' with its normal meaning, and expressing genuine belief in God with their assent to the sentence 'God exists.'

But now imagine a theist who finds this chain of reasoning plausible describing his view with the words

God exists, but the greatest possible being does not.

On the present proposal, this is synonymous with both of

The greatest possible being exists, but the greatest possible being does not.

God exists, but God does not.

But neither of these translations of the claim made by our mildly heterodox theist is remotely plausible. If this is not obvious, then the point can be pressed—as in the example of my five-year-old daughter—by noting that substitution of these sentences in the complement of an

---

attitude ascription with our heterodox theist as subject can change its truth-value.[26]

### 7.4.3 Impoverished modal space

In the preceding chapters we discussed a few examples of hypotheses about the universe which, if true, would 'shrink' modal space in an interesting way: they would make it the case that, although there is a greatest possible being, we would be strongly disinclined to think of that being as God. These sorts of hypotheses posed problems both for the conjunctive strategy for defending a pure alethic perfect being theology and for the attempt to use the principle that God is the greatest possible being to define the scope of 'permissible tinkering' with the concept of God. It is perhaps not entirely surprising that they also pose a problem for the view that 'God' is synonymous with 'the greatest possible being.'

To see why, recall the description of a 'Demosian' being in §2.4.1. Most, I take it, will be inclined to endorse the conditional

If a being is Demosian, that being is not God.

But it would be a mistake to endorse the thesis

If a being is Demosian, that being is not the greatest possible being.

Indeed, as we saw above, quite the opposite is true: if some being is Demosian, then that being *is* the greatest possible being. But if the two conditionals just stated can differ in truth-value, then 'God' and 'the greatest possible being' can't mean the same thing.

---

[26] Alston (1988), who defends the idea that 'God' is an ordinary name, also argues against descriptivist alternatives by considering the possibility of subjects who have 'wildly heterodox' views about God but nonetheless succeed in using the name to refer (122–3). The present argument is in the same spirit as his; the central difference is that (as the above examples illustrate) one need only use very mildly heterodox views to make trouble for perfect being semantics. I return to Alston's views about 'God' in Chapter 8.

Interestingly, Aquinas seems to have thought that even people with very radical theological views should count as believing in God. When criticizing the view that 'God' means 'that than which a greater cannot be thought', he remarks, 'After all, many ancients said that this world itself was God.' (*Summa Contra Gentiles* I.11).

The proponent of the view that 'God' is semantically equivalent to 'the greatest possible being' might be tempted to reply by modifying her position. Perhaps instead of being semantically equivalent to this simple description, 'God' is synonymous with some conjunctive description which requires its bearer to, in addition to being the greatest possible being, satisfy certain other conditions which a Demosian being would not satisfy.

But that is unlikely to help much. For one thing, it would worsen the problems discussed in §7.4.1 and §7.4.2, since it would increase rather than decrease the requirements on competent users of 'God.' And, relatedly, it would make cases of theological disagreement harder to come by than they should be, since genuine disagreement about God would seem to require parties to the disagreement to mean the same thing by 'God.' But as we pack extra conditions into the meaning of 'God,' we make it less and less likely that people with different views of the divine will all be using the term to refer to the same thing.[27]

### 7.4.4 'The greatest actual being'

It might seem that a move to the description 'the greatest actual being' could help the perfect being semanticist with some of the foregoing problems. For many of these problems turned on cases in which it is plausible that a subject believes that God exists without believing that 'the greatest possible being' is satisfied. But in each of these cases the subject does think that 'the greatest actual being' is satisfied.

But it does not take long to see that this virtue brings with it a disqualifying vice. This is just that many people who do not believe that God exists will be happy to endorse

The greatest actual being exists.

Take, for example, Bob, a garden variety atheist who thinks that everything which actually exists can be ranked according to greatness, and who thinks it very unlikely that there is an exact tie atop the greatness scale. It seems that

---

[27] See, for discussion, Sullivan (2015).

Bob believes that the greatest actual being exists.

will be true, despite

Bob believes that God exists.

being false. This shows (again, given plausible compositionality assumptions) that 'God' and 'the greatest actual being' are not semantically equivalent. This is, in a way, just an extreme version of the problem of impoverished modal space discussed in the preceding section, since the proponent of the idea that 'God' and 'the greatest actual being' are semantically equivalent takes the relevant modal space to include just one world.

We can conclude, I think, that 'God' is not a name like 'Goliath'; it does not simply abbreviate a description like 'the greatest possible being' or 'the greatest actual being.'

## 7.5 The modal conception and descriptive association

It is natural for the descriptivist at this point to fall back on the claim that 'the greatest possible being,' while not synonymous with 'God,' is nonetheless associated with 'God' in the sense that all competent speakers must be at least disposed to identify the reference of 'God' with the bearer of the property of being the greatest possible being. The arguments above, after all, relied on finding substitution failures involving the two terms. And, while this does discredit the view that 'the greatest possible being' is semantically equivalent to 'God,' it does not discredit the view that 'God' is description-associated, since (we are supposing) a name can be description-associated but still Millian.

But, while initially promising, this move does not in the end help much. Recall the example of the description-associated name 'Morton.' For this name to be description-associated was for all competent users of the name to associate the description with the name, and take the name to refer to the thing (if any) which uniquely satisfies the description. But the examples discussed in the previous section already show that 'God' cannot be description-associated in that way. Our unsophisticated and mildly heterodox speakers are competent users of the name, but don't associate 'the greatest possible being' with God. And those who entertain seriously any of the many modal-space-shrinking hypotheses discussed above will be inclined to doubt whether something bears the name 'God' just in case it is the greatest possible being, since they will take seriously hypotheses which entail that there is a greatest possible being who is not God.

## 7.6 The modal conception and descriptive introduction

Let's consider the last, weakest form of perfect being semantics, according to which 'God' is a Millian Kripkean name, but one which was introduced by the description 'greatest possible being' rather than by a dubbing.

The obvious problem with this view is just that it is wildly implausible that those who introduced the term (or its ancestors in other languages) tied it in this way to the modal conception of God. That conception is—relative to the use of names for the one god—of far too late a vintage. However exactly we understand the meaning of 'God,' terms with that meaning were used well before Boethius and Anselm appeared on the scene.[28]

In reply, the perfect being semanticist might point out that there is another way in which the reference of 'God' might depend on 'the greatest possible being,' without the latter having guided the original introduction of the name. This is a model which is more familiar from discussions of natural kind terms. Hilary Putnam observed that, in

---

[28] One might try to get around this worry by taking the relevant description to be 'the greatest actual being,' which is perhaps a more plausible candidate to have been in the minds of the speakers who introduced the ancestors of our term 'God.' But this would lead to a variant on the problem discussed in §7.4.4, which is that this would make the conditions on 'God' referring implausibly weak. Informed of the present theory of the description which fixes the reference of 'God,' our garden variety atheist will take 'God' to have a reference, and hence should endorse 'God exists.' But any theory of 'God' which has this consequence must be mistaken.

the case of natural kind terms like 'gold,' some speakers are competent users of the term even though not able reliably to identify instances of gold. Their ability to use 'gold' to nonetheless stand for the kind gold is due to the presence of others in their linguistic community who are able to recognize instances of the kind. Putnam then proposed a thesis, which he called the 'hypothesis of the universality of the division of linguistic labor':

> Every linguistic community . . . possesses at least some terms whose associated 'criteria' are known only to a subset of the speakers who acquire the terms, and whose use by the other speakers depends upon a structured cooperation between them and the speakers in the relevant subsets.[29]

Let's follow Putnam in distinguishing normal users of 'gold', who are not able to reliably identify instances of the kind, from experts, who can. Putnam is not proposing that 'gold' out of the mouths of normal users has its reference determined by the way in which 'gold' was introduced in the past; he is proposing that it is determined by the practices of experts, who are (in the simplest case) contemporaries of the relevant normal users. Often it is said that this is explained by the fact that normal users are disposed to *defer* in their usage of the relevant term to the experts. There are serious and under-explored problems with understanding what this relation of deference amounts to;[30] but for now let's just suppose that the standard story

---

[29] Putnam (1973), 706.

[30] On the one hand, deference is often glossed in such a way that the relation is very undemanding—so one might say, for example, that A defers to B with respect to expression e simply in virtue of A intending to use e with the same meaning as B does. But this relation is so undemanding that it does not guarantee asymmetry, and so does not explain why the non-expert's use of e inherits the expert's use, rather than the other way around. Experts, after all, might also have intentions to use the term with the same meaning as non-experts.

To avoid this problem, one might make the relation more demanding, and that A have an appropriately 'deferential' attitude toward B—by, for example, being willing to accept correction from B with respect to the use of e. But then it is implausible that we'll be able to cover all of the cases that need to be covered, because A may be, just as a matter of temperament, disposed to accept correction from no one—and an expert might be, again just as a matter of temperament, extremely conflict-averse and concessive when it comes to discussions about the extensions of the terms with respect to which he is expert. See, for discussion, Burge (1986) and Greenberg (2001).

is right, and that in at least many cases natural kind terms out of the mouths of normal users have their reference determined by the content of that term out of the mouths of the experts to whom the normal users defer. Might 'God' have its reference determined by theological experts in the way that 'gold' is claimed to have its reference determined by scientific experts?

Even if this general model were applicable to 'God', though, there is little hope that the description 'the greatest possible being' would play a role in determining its reference. If we extend the Putnam model, perhaps the theological experts would be practicing theologians and persons in positions of religious authority. But it does not seem especially likely that most, or even many, of these people would be inclined to explicitly link the reference of 'God' to 'the greatest possible being', as opposed to other descriptions. Of course, a fairly large number of contemporary analytic philosophers of religion may be so inclined; but it is difficult to see what mechanism would explain the reference of 'God' out of the mouths of normal users being inherited from this select group.

\*   \*   \*

At this stage, we face a kind of dilemma. On the one hand, we have two arguments for the conclusion that 'God' is not an ordinary name, and three versions of perfect being semantics which promise to explain the sense in which 'God' is not an ordinary name. But, on closer examination, none of these versions of perfect being semantics seem to be tenable. This leaves us with an unanswered question: how are we to understand the meaning of 'God'?

So the failure of perfect being semantics—like the failure of the constructive program of perfect being theology and the failure of the perfect being defense—leaves us with an unanswered question. In the next chapter, I make some first steps at addressing these questions from a perspective very different from the one given to us by perfect being theology.

# 8

# Beyond Perfect Being Theology

We've now considered three different questions which the principle that God is the greatest possible being has been used to answer:

- What are the divine attributes?
- Which properties are non-negotiable, core parts of our concept of God?
- What is the meaning of 'God'?

In none of these cases does the principle that God is the greatest possible being provide the answers we want. The modal conception of God is not, unfortunately, the productive first principle for philosophical theology that it is often taken to be.

This raises the natural question: where do we go from here? In this last chapter I want to make a few suggestions.

## 8.1 Deriving the attributes

Attempts to derive the attributes are attempts to argue for a claim of the form

God is $F$.

Typically, if one wants to derive the truth of a monadic predication like this one, one needs a premise which attributes some other property to the being in question. So, if we want to argue for some claim of the above sort, we need a premise which attributes some other property to God, from which we can go on to derive other claims about the divine attributes. Let's call properties ascribed by premises of this sort *foundational attributes*. Then the central methodological question for attempts to derive the divine attributes is: where do we find our foundational attributes?

The answer given by at least many advocates of perfect being theology would be: we get the key foundational attribute from the concept of God, which is the concept of a greatest possible being. We then use the claim that God has this property—the one ascribed by [GPB]—to show that God must be omnipotent, omniscient, etc. I've argued that this attempt is a failure. Where else might we look for foundational attributes?

One traditional way to find foundational attributes is from natural theology. This method begins with an existence proof: a proof that there exists some being which is *F*. It is then argued that a being which is *F* must also be *G*, that a being which is *F* and *G* must also be *H*, and so on until we have a collection of attributes such that it is plausible that the bearer of those attributes is God. One finds this method in, among many other authors, Aquinas, where the existence proof establishes the existence of an unmoved mover, and then it is argued that an unmoved mover must be eternal, fully actual, and simple.[1]

In a way, we can see Anselm's strategy as a special case of this more general one: it's just that Anselm's existence proof is the ontological argument, which gives him the property of being the greatest conceivable being as his foundational attribute. This is thus the special case in which the methods of perfect being theology and natural theology overlap. I suspect, though, that at least many contemporary perfect being theologians would be less comfortable locating themselves in the tradition of natural theology, because many would be skeptical about the ontological argument's ability to establish the

---

[1] See *Summa Contra Gentiles* I.13–18. For a nice overview, see Chapter 4 of Shields and Pasnau (2016). I should note that Aquinas does sometimes reason in a way more similar to the method of the perfect being theologian, as at *Summa Theologica* Ia, q. 4. Thanks to Therese Cory for pointing this out to me.

conclusion that the property of being the greatest conceivable being is instantiated. But, even setting worries about the ontological argument to the side, we've seen in Chapters 2–4 that taking being the greatest possible (or conceivable) being as a foundational attribute doesn't in the end enable us to derive anything of significance about the divine attributes.

A second traditional way to find foundational attributes is via what Aquinas calls the science of sacred doctrine. This science

does not argue in proof of its principles, which are the articles of faith, but from them it goes on to prove something else, as the Apostle from the resurrection of Christ argues in proof of the general resurrection.[2]

This method gets its starting point from revealed claims about God, and derives further claims from these.

I think that it is reasonably clear why contemporary perfect being theologians want a third option. Many, I suspect, are skeptical of the traditional arguments for the existence of God—or at least don't want their work in philosophical theology to be hostage to the success of these arguments. But despite this skepticism about natural theology, I think that many contemporary philosophers share the aspiration of the natural theologian to derive claims about God without the use of claims from revelation, and hence without engaging in the science of sacred doctrine.[3]

One can think of the sort of perfect being theologian who is skeptical about natural theology as attempting to do rational theology in the absence of natural theology, by trying to extract a foundational attribute from the very concept of God. The hope was to find a way to reason about the attributes while, in a sense, bracketing questions about the success of arguments for the existence of God. The perfect being theologian gets her foundational attribute—the property of being the greatest possible, or conceivable, being—not from the

---

[2] *Summa Theologica* Ia.q1.a8.

[3] Though some delicacy is called for here, since many perfect being theologians are happy to think of their work on the divine attributes as constrained by revealed doctrine. See, for instance, the discussion of Leftow's 'Scriptural perfect being theology' in §4.2.

existence proofs of the natural theologian, but just from examination of the concept of God.

We have seen that the concept of God is not the modal conception of God and that, even if it were, it is not easy to see how to derive anything of interest from it. But even if these negative conclusions are correct, it is worth asking whether some other version of the perfect being theologian's 'third option' might fare better. Might some other analysis of the concept of God give us the foundational attributes we seek?

I doubt it. This is not because there is nothing to the concept of God; as we have seen from our examples of impoverished modal space, there are genuinely constraints on what a thing would have to be like in order to count as the referent of 'God'.[4] But I doubt that the concept of God is anywhere near determinate enough to yield meaty conceptual truths which might enable us to get started deriving non-trivial results about the attributes, as it might if 'God' were simply synonymous with a description like 'the greatest possible being'. Disputes about whether some property or another is really part of the concept of God are thus likely to be simply verbal.

Suppose that we can get our foundational attributes neither from the modal conception of God nor from the existence proofs characteristic of natural theology. It is then hard to see how we can get started theorizing about the attributes of God without bringing to bear substantial assumptions about God which are themselves neither conceptual truths nor knowable by reason alone. It seems inevitable then that our reasoning about the attributes of God will be somewhat parochial, in the sense that it will be guided by theses about God which not all believers in God will be willing to endorse. But these need not be quite as specific as, for example, the claim that Christ rose from the dead.

For instance, one might take as one's foundational attribute the property of being capable of offering human beings genuine salvation; or the property of being a suitable object of faith; or the property of being deserving of worship. (Though we should not pretend that the

---

[4] More on this in §8.3 below.

claims that God has these properties are conceptual truths.) Of course, properties like these do already play a role in theorizing about the attributes in contemporary philosophy of religion. But a philosophical theology which put properties like these, rather than the property of being the greatest possible being, at the center would look quite a bit different.[5]

## 8.2 Dispensable vs. mandatory attributes

Let's turn now to our second unanswered question: the question of how we distinguish dispensable from mandatory candidate divine attributes. This was the distinction between those attributes which may, and those which may not, reasonably be denied by a theist to hold of God. An answer to this question is something very much worth wanting. It is also prima facie quite plausible that we should be able to derive such a criterion from the conception of God as the greatest possible, or the greatest conceivable, being. But, as we saw in Chapter 6, the attempt to find such a criterion seems to be a failure.

It would be depressing if this made the sort of dialectic between theist and atheist described in Chapter 6 wholly unprincipled. But the failure of the perfect being defense need not quite have this dire consequence. It does, however, suggest that the debate between the theist and the non-theist should be, in a certain way, reconceived.

As mentioned in the previous section, it seems to me unlikely that there is any principle which can—as [Conditions] tries to—neatly state, in a way which avoids substantial theological assumptions, the conditions under which God would exist. But this is in a way wholly unremarkable. For consider other philosophical debates about existence—for example, debates about whether anything really has free will, whether things are really colored, and whether abstract

---

[5] An example of someone who puts considerations like these front and center is Geach (1973). The contrast in focus between that piece and more recent discussions of omnipotence which are guided by the modal conception of God is significant.

objects exist. In none of these cases is it easy to come up with a simple, non-trivial biconditional of the form

$x$ has free will iff . . .

which is acceptable to all parties.

Despite this, debates about free will (and the other topics just mentioned) are not completely unprincipled. This is in part because there is some agreement about particular cases—a fact which would not seem to have an analogue in the debate between theist and non-theist. But it is also in part because participants in debates about, for example, the existence of free will have tried to structure them by connecting these debates to the sorts of questions that made us care about free will in the first place—like questions about moral responsibility and praiseworthiness.

A similar move can be used to structure the debate between theist and non-theist, by focusing on attributes like those discussed in the preceding section. When we are asking whether some property is dispensable, we can ask questions like: could a being without this property offer salvation to human beings? Or: could a being without this property be a suitable object of the absolute trust characteristic of religious faith? Or: could a being without this property be deserving of worship?

This is of course not an entirely new idea. van Inwagen, for example, raises precisely this sort of question when discussing the consequences of the denial that God can know which future free actions agents will perform. He asks,

If one believes that human beings have free will and that God does not know how human beings will act when they act freely, does this not imply that God was not in a position to make the promises that (Christians believe) God has in fact made?[6]

Questions like this, it seems to me, should guide our views about which candidate attributes should be regarded as dispensable and which mandatory.

[6] van Inwagen (2008), 228.

Of course, this sort of approach incorporates substantial assumptions about God: that God does offer us genuine salvation, that God is deserving of trust and worship, and that God is the kind of being which makes promises. Not all believers in God share these assumptions, and so not all believers in God should focus on just these kinds of questions as informing their views about the mandatory/dispensable distinction. For this reason, the present rec-ommendation has the consequence that the ground rules for debates about the existence of God—that is, our criterion for distinguishing mandatory from dispensable attributes—may well vary depending upon the particular theological views of the theist in question.

One might worry that this gives at least some debates in the phi-losophy of religion less generality than we might ideally like them to have. But that, I think, is preferable to relying on the principle that God is the greatest possible being to play a role which, if the argument of Chapter 6 is correct, it is most unsuited to play.

## 8.3 The meaning of 'God'

Let's turn at last to our question about the meaning of 'God.' We saw in Chapter 7 that reasonable arguments suggest that 'God' is not an ordinary name; but we also saw that the various versions of perfect being semantics do not provide an especially plausible alternative model.

### 8.3.1 'God' as an ordinary name

As a first step forward, let's re-examine our three arguments against simply treating 'God' as an ordinary name. None, I think, are as effective as they at first seem.

#### 8.3.1.1 THE ABSENCE OF DUBBINGS

If 'God' is an ordinary name, then it must have been introduced by a dubbing; but, Johnston argues there is no one original dubbing that we can hope to fall back on, nothing at all akin to the introduction of a name for a person. How then should we understand the way in which the name was introduced?

Answering this question will obviously involve some historical speculation. But I think that we can at least imagine one way in which things might have gone. Richard Miller suggests that the name 'God' has multiple contexts of introduction:

'God' is multiply grounded in direct references. The Judeo-Christian understanding of history is that God has repeatedly encountered man, in the prophets of the Old Testament and beyond. Others would add that God directly encounters many anonymous men and women in their daily lives in the present as well as in the past. . . . [7]

Let's suppose that this 'Judeo-Christian understanding of history' is correct. Then the occasions in which God has encountered human beings could have put the particular human beings encountered in a position to have thoughts about God. They could then introduce a name (the ancestor of 'God') for the being encountered. This model is consistent with some of the apparent encounters being illusory, so long as one being is involved in most, or perhaps almost all, of the encounters. The name introduced could then, for all we have said, be a dubbing-introduced Millian name for that being, and its path from its introduction until the present could fit the standard model of a Kripkean name.

This gives us at least the beginnings of a way in which we might understand 'God' as dubbing-introduced.

### 8.3.1.2 REQUIREMENTS ON REFERENCE

The argument from requirements on reference argued that 'God' cannot be an ordinary name for whatever the original users of the name had in mind, because, if they were radically deceived about the nature of the being with whom they were in contact (as in the 'joker' example), the name would not refer.

---

[7] Miller (1986), 11–12.

Curiously, Alston uses very similar examples to argue for the exact opposite conclusion, that 'God' is an ordinary name:

First, suppose that an impostor—the devil, one's internalized father figure, or whatever—represents himself as God. We are to imagine someone who, like the Old Testament prophets, takes himself to be addressed by God, to be given commissions by God, and so on. But, unlike the Old Testament prophets, as they have traditionally been regarded, our chap is really being addressed by Satan; or else some internalized figure from his past is responsible for the 'messages.' To make this the kind of case we want we must suppose that this impostor represents himself as the true God, creator of heaven and earth, righteous judge, merciful redeemer, and so on.... I think the right thing to say here is that our dupe is really speaking of Satan when he says 'God told me to put all unbelievers to the sword'.... Moreover if a community grows up on the basis of these revelations and epiphanies, and the practice develops in that community of using 'God' to refer to the focus of the worship of the community, we will have a Satan worshipping community in which the members use the name 'God' for Satan.[8]

This suggests that Alston would respond to the example imagined by Sobel by simply biting the bullet: in that scenario, 'God' would refer to the joker.

While this view of the case is certainly consistent with the view that 'God' is an ordinary name, it is not especially credible. For consider one of Alston's examples, in which 'an internalized figure from one's past' is responsible for all of the instances in which (for example) Christians take human beings to have come in contact with God. And suppose further that there is no great being which created the universe and everything in it; suppose, that is, that the universe is much as standard sorts of atheists think that it is. Alston's view would have us say that, in that case, when Christians say 'God exists,' they speak truly. After all, we can suppose that the relevant 'internalized figures from the past' really do exist, and that, on Alston's view, is enough for 'God' to refer. But that seems clearly incorrect. In that scenario, atheism is true, and hence 'God exists' is false; but then in that scenario, contra Alston, 'God' must lack a reference.

---

[8] Alston (1988), 121.

Alston may reply by conceding that, were that scenario actual, 'God' as *we* use it would lack a reference. But this does not immediately entail that 'God' as used by members of the community described would lack a reference.

But, while this reply is correct as far as it goes, it is just not at all credible that 'God' out of the mouths of members of the community would refer. For surely if they were to learn the truth of their situation, they would conclude, correctly, that atheism is true and so could correctly say in their own language, 'God does not exist.'

So Alston's response to the problem should be rejected. A much better response to problematic scenarios of this sort is suggested in an insightful paper by Jerome I. Gellman. He considers the following example:

I am at the zoo with my children. We have been giving funny-sounding names to individual animals all afternoon. Late in the afternoon, I sight what I, and my kids, think is a smallish animal off in the grass of the Australian display, and I dub it with the name 'Kuzu.' Just for fun. On coming closer to the Australian pavilion we discover that what I thought was an animal was merely a pile of soiled rags, bearing the configuration of a kind of funny-looking animal.... Upon discovering the pile of rags, I would not say that Kuzu ... turned out to be a configuration of rags, or the rags themselves....

It's true that at the zoo that day we never made any explicit rule to the effect that we would name only animals. Nonetheless, that was the game we were playing, and it was implicitly understood that we were giving funny names to animals. By virtue of the focus of the naming it was understood that only animals would get such names.... Rags held no interest for us, neither at the zoo nor anywhere else, and there was no point or purpose or fun in giving a name to them. 'Kuzu' just wasn't the name of anything, even though I thought it was.[9]

What this example brings out is that, even in perfectly ordinary cases of dubbing-introduced names, there are constraints on the sort of thing that can be dubbed. These constraints are often implicit, but no less real for that. So the fact that 'God' could not name Sobel's joker,

---

[9] Gellman (1995), 537–8.

or Alston's 'internalized figure,' is perfectly consistent with 'God' being an ordinary dubbing-introduced name.

We might of course go on to ask what the relevant constraints on reference are. In the case of 'Kuzu,' the constraint is that it can name only animals. What is the corresponding rule for 'God'?

The perfect being semanticist might propose that the corresponding rule for 'God' is that the name is constrained to refer only to the greatest possible being. But the examples given above show that this hypothesis is false for at least three reasons: (i) those who introduced the name (or its ancestors) are very unlikely to have had this description, even implicitly, in mind; (ii) arguments for the impossibility of there being a greatest possible being suggest that it is at least conceivable that something be the referent of 'God' without satisfying this description; and (iii) our examples of impoverished modal space suggest that something can satisfy the description without being the referent of 'God.'

Gellman suggests instead, adapting the views of Robert Nozick, that 'God' is constrained to refer only to something which is

(1) the most perfect actual being,
(2) who is very high on the scale of perfection,
(3) whose perfection is vastly greater than that of the second most perfect actual being, and
(4) upon whom all other beings in some important way depend.[10]

As a constraining description, this seems to fare better than 'the greatest possible being.' This is because (i) it is not implausible that early users of the name had, at least implicitly, something of this sort in mind, (ii) it is satisfiable even if it is impossible that there be a greatest possible being, and (iii) it is not satisfied in the scenarios of impoverished modal space we've described.[11]

---

[10] Gellman (1995), 542. For Nozick's discussion, see Nozick (1989), 46–54.

[11] Once we have introduced the idea of a constraining description, one might think that this could be used to formulate the thing I claimed we could not formulate in the preceding section: a criterion for distinguishing mandatory from dispensable attributes. For can't we say that an attribute is dispensable iff denying that it is instantiated it does not entail that the description just laid out is unsatisfied? In a sense,

Summing up: even dubbing-introduced names are descriptively constrained. And if we take 'God' to be a dubbing-introduced ordinary name which is descriptively constrained in the way just sketched, the argument from requirements on reference dissolves.

### 8.3.1.3 INFORMATIVE IDENTITIES

Let's consider now the last of our three arguments, the argument from informative identities. Johnston pointed out that if we take 'Yahweh' to be a dubbing-introduced ordinary name, we can imagine someone, as Marcion did, coherently wondering whether Yahweh is God. And indeed we can imagine the same for any ordinary name.

An initial response to this argument is to point out that, for any pair of ordinary names, one can coherently wonder whether they refer to the same thing. So, to take the stock example of 'Hesperus' and 'Phosphorus,' competent speakers can coherently wonder whether Hesperus is Phosphorus. Given this datum, one might then wonder why the fact that Marcion could coherently wonder whether Yahweh is God should tell at all against the hypothesis that both 'God' and 'Yahweh' are ordinary dubbing-introduced names.[12]

Against this hypothesis, a proponent of Johnston's argument might object that, while it does make room for Marcion's doubt, it mischaracterizes the nature of that doubt. For surely Marcion was not *just* doubting whether two dubbing-introduced names were introduced

---

I think that this line of thought is unobjectionable; but, in practice, it is unlikely to give us a criterion which is at all useful. This is because the constraining description in this case is so vague as to give us basically no guidance in cases of interest about whether the attribute is dispensable or not. For example, can a being which lacks omniscience be high enough on the scale of perfection? Our description does not tell us; neither, I think, does anything else in 'the concept of God.'

[12] More cautiously, it certainly seems as though 'wonder whether Hesperus is Phosphorus' describes something which competent speakers can coherently do. Many Millians will deny that what these speakers are really coherently doing is truly described as wondering whether Hesperus is Phosphorus, this (on the Millian view in question) being the same thing as wondering whether Hesperus is Hesperus. But even on this kind of view the argument from informative identities would seem to be in trouble, for the same diagnosis of the case of Marcion will be available.

as names for the same being; his was a distinctively theological doubt about the properties of the bearer of the name 'Yahweh.'

But the model just sketched suggests two replies. The first is just that the ancient astronomer who doubts whether Hesperus is really Phosphorus is not just doubting whether two dubbing-introduced names were introduced as names for the same being; his is a distinctively astronomical doubt about the properties of the bearers of the relevant names. So again it is not clear that we have any disanalogy between 'God' and ordinary names.[13]

The second reply emphasizes the fact that 'God' is, even if dubbing-introduced, descriptively constrained in the way that Gellman suggests. Given this, the question of whether Yahweh is God can be understood as asking whether Yahweh has the properties which constrain candidates for the reference of 'God.'

### 8.3.2 The real problem with 'God' as an ordinary name

Despite these points, I don't think that in the end the hypothesis that 'God' is an ordinary name—even one whose dubbing was descriptively constrained in the way that Gellman suggests—can be sustained. This is because there seem to be certain descriptions of the world which are coherent, but would be incoherent if 'God' were an ordinary name. Here is an example of the sort of thing I have in mind:

God exists and created the world and everything in it. But God stayed remote from God's creation, and in particular never directly encountered any human being. No one has ever in any sense perceived God, or communicated with God.

It seems to me that this is a perfectly coherent view; it is not far off of the view which some classical deists seem to have had. Further, it seems to me, someone might hold this view while being a perfectly competent user of the name 'God.'

---

[13] One can of course wonder how the proponent of the thesis that 'Hesperus' and 'Phosphorus' are ordinary names can explain the distinctively astronomical character of the astronomer's doubt. For one kind of response, see Soames (2002).

But this is difficult to understand if 'God' really is dubbing-introduced. For if 'God' is dubbing-introduced, then introducers of the name must have had some prior way of making singular reference to the bearer of the name. And if God stays remote from creation, and never encounters any human being via perception or communication, how could introducers of the name have secured such original reference, if not indirectly via description?

Compare this to a genuinely dubbing-introduced name, like my daughter's name 'Violet.' I cannot coherently entertain the hypothesis that Violet exists, but has never encountered either me or my wife in any way. The same goes for Gellman's example of 'Kuzu.' He and his kids could not coherently entertain the hypothesis that Kuzu exists, but did not encounter them in any way.

This suggests that 'God' is not a dubbing-introduced ordinary name, but is rather descriptively introduced. It is, in this respect, like 'Neptune.' But, for the reasons discussed above, the relevant description is not 'the greatest possible being.' Instead, I suggest, it is something along the lines of the complex description provided by Nozick. In this respect, 'God' does diverge from the model of an ordinary name. But this difference in the way that the name was introduced does not imply that the name is either non-Kripkean or non-Millian.[14] Quite the opposite: attempts to incorporate the descriptive condition derived from Nozick into either the semantic content of the name or its competence conditions would be open to close relatives of the arguments deployed against perfect being semantics in Chapter 7.

\* \* \*

If the argument of this book is correct, then at the root of perfect being theology are two fundamental errors.

The first is the error of thinking that the thesis that God is the greatest possible being can lead us to a more specific understanding

---

[14] One might object that names introduced via description, rather than some sort of acquaintance, cannot be devices of direct reference. For criticism of this sort of acquaintance-based criterion for singular thought, see Hawthorne and Manley (2012).

of God. The thesis is powerless to do this without modal assumptions equivalent to the claims about God for which we wanted to argue.

The second is the error of thinking that the concept of God just is the modal conception of God. This is mistaken on two levels. The first is in thinking that our concept of God is this empty; something could satisfy this formal characterization, and be the best thing in some space of suitably grim worlds, and yet not be the sort of thing which could qualify as God. The second is in thinking that the concept of God is neat enough that conceptual truths about God might be a genuine starting point for thinking about God, one which is distinct both from the tradition of natural theology and the science of sacred doctrine.

Any path forward has to begin with assumptions about God which are more substantial, in two senses, than what is given by the modal conception of God. First, it must say something more specific about what God is like, something more than the bare claim that God is the best thing in some space of worlds. Second, in so doing, it will go beyond anything which could credibly be claimed to be a simple unpacking of the concept of God.

Where should we get these assumptions? My suggestion has been that we return to the reason why questions about the nature and existence of God are of such fundamental importance. This is the question of what it would take for there to be a being to whom it makes sense to say, 'you have made us for yourself, and our hearts are restless until they rest in you.'[15]

---

[15] Augustine, *Confessions* I.1.

# References

Robert Merrihew Adams, 1994. *Leibniz: Determinist, Theist, Idealist*. Oxford University Press.

Robert Merrihew Adams, 1999. *Finite and Infinite Goods: A Framework for Ethics*. Oxford University Press.

Michael J. Almeida, 2014. *The Metaphysics of Perfect Beings*. Routledge.

William P. Alston, 1988. Referring to God. *International Journal for Philosophy of Religion* 24(3):113–28.

St. Anselm, 2008. *Anselm of Canterbury: The Major Works*. Oxford University Press.

Alan Berger, 2002. *Terms and Truth: Reference Direct and Anaphoric*. Bradford.

Michael Bergmann and J. A. Cover, 2006. Divine Responsibility Without Divine Freedom. *Faith and Philosophy* 23(4):381–408.

Boethius, 1897. *The Consolation of Philosophy*. Elliot Stock.

Tyler Burge, 1986. Intellectual Norms and the Foundations of Mind. *Journal of Philosophy*, 83(12):697–720.

J. P. Burgess, 2014. Madagascar Revisited. *Analysis* 74(2):195–201.

David J. Chalmers, 2012. *Constructing the World*. Oxford University Press.

David J. Chalmers, 2002. Does Conceivability Entail Possibility? In *Conceivability and Possibility*, edited by Tamar S. Gendler and John Hawthorne, 145–200. Oxford University Press.

Andrew Chignell and Dean Zimmerman, 2012. Review of *Saving God*, by Mark Johnston. *Books and Culture*.

John Cottingham, Robert Stoothoff, Dugald Murdoch, and Anthony Kenny, 1988. *Descartes: Selected Philosophical Writings*. Cambridge University Press.

Richard Cross, 2005. *Duns Scotus on God*. Ashgate.

Gareth Evans, 1973. The Causal Theory of Names. *Aristotelian Society Supplementary Volume* 47(1):187–208.

Gareth Evans, 1982. *The Varieties of Reference*. Oxford University Press.

Thomas P. Flint, 1983. The Problem of Divine Freedom. *American Philosophical Quarterly*, 20(3):255–64.

Thomas P. Flint and Alfred J. Freddoso, 1983. Maximal power. In *The Existence and Nature of God*, edited by Alfred J. Freddoso, 81–113. University of Notre Dame Press.

Harry Frankfurt, 1977. Descartes on the Creation of the Eternal Truths. *Philosophical Review* 86(1):36–57.

P. T. Geach, 1973. Omnipotence. *Philosophy* 48(183):7–20.

Jerome I. Gellman, 1995. The Name of God. *Noûs* 29(4):536–43.

Mark Greenberg, 2001. *Thoughts Without Masters: Incomplete Understanding and the Content of Mind*. Dissertation, Oxford University.

Theodore Guleserian, 1983. God and Possible Worlds: The Modal Problem of Evil. *Noûs* 17(2):221–38.

James F. Harris, 1991. The Causal Theory of Reference and Religious Language. *International Journal for Philosophy of Religion* 29(2):75–86.

Charles Hartshorne, 1962. *The Logic of Perfection*. Open Court Pub. Co.

John Hawthorne and David Manley, 2012. *The Reference Book*. Oxford University Press.

Daniel Hill, 2004. *Divinity and Maximal Greatness*. Routledge.

Joshua Hoffman and Gary S. Rosenkrantz, 2008. *The Divine Attributes*. Wiley-Blackwell.

Daniel Howard-Snyder and Frances Howard-Snyder, 1994. How an Unsurpassable Being Can Create a Surpassable World. *Faith and Philosophy* 11(2):260–8.

David Hume, 2000 [1739]. *A Treatise of Human Nature*. Oxford University Press.

Mark Johnston, 2011. *Saving God: Religion After Idolatry*. Princeton University Press.

Dan Kaufman, 2002. Descartes's Creation Doctrine and Modality. *Australasian Journal of Philosophy* 80(1):24–41.

Saul Kripke, 1972. *Naming and Necessity*. Harvard University Press.

Brian Leftow, 2004. Anselm's Perfect Being Theology. In *The Cambridge Companion to Anselm*, edited by Brian Leftow, 132–56. Cambridge University Press.

Brian Leftow, 2011. Why Perfect Being Theology? *International Journal for Philosophy of Religion* 69(2):103–18.

Brian Leftow, 2012. *God and Necessity*. Oxford University Press.

Brian Leftow, 2015. Perfection and Possibility. *Faith and Philosophy* 32(4):423–31.

Gottfried Leibniz, 1969. *Philosophical Papers and Letters*. Reidel, 2nd edition.

Peter Lewis, 2001. Why The Pessimistic Induction Is A Fallacy. *Synthese* 129(3):371–80.

George I. Mavrodes, 1963. Some Puzzles Concerning Omnipotence. *Philosophical Review* 72(2):221–3.

John McDowell, 1977. On the Sense and Reference of a Proper Name. *Mind* 86(342):159–85.

Richard B. Miller, 1986. The Reference of 'God'. *Faith and Philosophy* 3(1):3–15.

Thomas V. Morris, 1987. Perfect Being Theology. *Noûs* 21(1):19–30.

Thomas V. Morris, 1983. Impeccability. *Analysis* 43(2):106–12.

Thomas V. Morris, 1985. The Necessity of God's Goodness. *New Scholasticism* 59(4):418–48. Reprinted in Morris (1989), 42–69.

Thomas V. Morris, 1987. *The Concept of God*. Oxford University Press.

Thomas V. Morris, 1989. *Anselmian Explorations: Essays in Philosophical Theology*. University of Notre Dame Press.

Thomas V. Morris, 1991. *Our Idea of God: An Introduction to Philosophical Theology*. Intervarsity Press.

Wes Morriston, 2001. Omnipotence and Necessary Moral Perfection: Are They Compatible? *Religious Studies* 37(2):143–60.

Wesley Morriston, 1985. Is God 'Significantly Free'?. *Faith and Philosophy* 2(3):257–64.

Michael J. Murray and Michael C. Rea, 2008. *An Introduction to the Philosophy of Religion*. Cambridge University Press.

Yujin Nagasawa, 2008. A New Defence of Anselmian Theism. *Philosophical Quarterly* 58(233):577–96.

Yujin Nagasawa, 2013. Models of Anselmian Theism. *Faith and Philosophy* 30(1):3–25.

S. Newlands, 2013. Leibniz and the Ground of Possibility. *Philosophical Review* 122(2):155–87.

Robert Nozick, 1989. *The Examined Life: Philosophical Meditations*. Simon & Schuster.

Graham Oppy, 2011. Perfection, Near-Perfection, Maximality, and Anselmian Theism. *International Journal for Philosophy of Religion* 69(2):119–38.

Nelson Pike, 1969. Omnipotence and God's Ability to Sin. *American Philosophical Quarterly* 6(3):208–16.

Alvin Plantinga and Patrick Grim, 1993. Truth, Omniscience, and Cantorian Arguments: An Exchange. *Philosophical Studies* 71:267–306.

Plato, 1908. *Republic*. Clarendon, 3rd edition.

Hilary Putnam, 1973. Meaning and Reference. *Journal of Philosophy* 70(19):699–711.

Michael C. Rea, 2016. Hiddenness and Transcendence. In *Hidden Divinity and Religious Belief*, edited by Adam Green and Eleanore Stump, 210–25. Cambridge University Press.

Lawrence Resnick, 1973. God and the Best Possible World. *American Philosophical Quarterly* 10(4):313–17.

Katherin A. Rogers, 2000. *Perfect Being Theology*. Edinburgh University Press.

William L. Rowe, 2004. *Can God Be Free?* Clarendon Press.

G. Schlesinger, 1964. The Problem of Evil and the Problem of Suffering. *American Philosophical Quarterly* 1(3):244–7.

Duns Scotus, 1987. *Duns Scotus: Philosophical Writings.* Hackett Publishing Company.

Wilfrid S. Sellars, 1962. Philosophy and the Scientific Image of Man. In *Science, Perception, and Reality,* edited by Robert Colodny, 35–78. Humanities Press.

Christopher Shields and Robert Pasnau, 2016. *The Philosophy of Aquinas.* Oxford University Press.

Scott Soames, 2002. *Beyond Rigidity: The Unfinished Semantic Agenda of Naming and Necessity.* Oxford University Press.

Jordan Howard Sobel, 2004. *Logic and Theism: Arguments for and Against Beliefs in God.* Cambridge University Press.

Jeff Speaks, 2010. Epistemic Two-Dimensionalism and the Epistemic Argument. *Australasian Journal of Philosophy* 88(1):59–78.

Jeff Speaks, 2014. The Method of Perfect Being Theology. *Faith and Philosophy* 31(3):256–66.

Meghan Sullivan, 2015. The Semantic Problem of Hiddenness. In *Hidden Divinity and Religious Belief: New Perspectives,* edited by Adam Green and Eleonore Stump, 35–52. Cambridge University Press.

James van Cleve, 1983. Conceivability and the Cartesian Argument for Dualism. *Pacific Philosophical Quarterly* 64(January):35–45.

Peter van Inwagen, 1991. The Problem of Evil, the Problem of Air, and the Problem of Silence. *Philosophical Perspectives* 5:135–65.

Peter van Inwagen, 2006. *The Problem of Evil.* Clarendon Press.

Peter van Inwagen, 2008. What Does an Omniscient Being Know About the Future? In *Oxford Studies in Philosophy of Religion,* edited by Jonathan L. Kvanvig, 216–30. Oxford University Press.

Edward Wierenga, 2001. Timelessness Out of Mind: On the Alleged Incoherence of Divine Timelessness. *In God and Time: Essays on the Divine Nature,* edited by Gregory E. Ganssle and David M. Woodruff, 153–64. Oxford University Press.

John Worrall, 1989. Structural Realism: The Best of Both Worlds? *Dialectica* 43(1–2):99–124.

Stephen Yablo, 1993. Is Conceivability a Guide to Possibility? *Philosophy and Phenomenological Research* 53(1):1–42.

# Index